BUDDHISM MADE PLAIN

An Introduction for Christians and Jews

Revised Edition

ANTONY FERNANDO

**WITH
LEONARD SWIDLER**

ABOUT IPUBCLOUD.COM

iPubCloud.com is the Digital Publishing arm of iPub Global Connection, LLC. Focused on globally transformative books from authors all over the world, we value creators who seek to influence our world in matters of equality, inter-religious dialogue, and planet sustainability.

Our value to you is simplicity and convenience. The continually curated book list is culled from the New York Times, Amazon reader reviews and iPub subject matter advisors. You may be confident when you select an item from our store; everything is fulfilled by Amazon, its affiliates, and other important distribution channels.

There are many books like this one on iPubCloud.com along with selections of other types of books. Don't keep us a secret. Connect with us on Facebook and join our mailing list.

iPub Global Connection, LLC
www.iPubCloud.com
550 W. Baseline Rd., #303
Mesa, AZ 85210
info@iPubCloud.com

Cover Design by Arewa Abiodun Ibrahim
Photo Credit: Tooykrub/shutterstock.com

ISBN-13: 978-1-948575-02-7 Kindle
ISBN-13: 978-1-948575-03-4 Paperback

Contents

PART TWO

HUMAN LIBERATION:
THE INNER AFFINITY
AMONG THE VIEWS OF GAUTAMA, YESHUA, AND
JUDAISM

Abbreviations Used for
Buddhist Scriptural Sources

AN   *Anguttara Nikaya* (followed by reference to the volume and page of the Pali text)

CV   *Cullavagga of the Vinaya Pitaka* (followed by reference to the page, chapter, section, and verse of the Pali text)

DN   *Digha Nikaya* (followed by reference to the number of the Sutta)

MN   *Majjhima Nikaya* (followed by reference to the volume and page of the Pali text)

MV   *Mahavagga of the Vinaya Pitaka* (followed by reference to the page, chapter, section, and verse of the Pali text)

SN   *Samyutta Nikaya* (followed by reference to the volume and page of the Pali text)

VP   *Vinaya Pitaka* (cited through MV or CV)

English translations are from the editions of the Pali Text Society, London.

Buddhist Terms in Pali

Buddhism, like any other religion, has a vocabulary all its own and its more cherished words and expressions are taken from the foundational scriptures. Among the languages in which the Buddhist scriptures are set down, Pali is one of the most important. Many technical terms in Buddhism—and almost all the terms in the Theravada form of Buddhism—are in Pali. A number of these Pali terms and expressions are included in this exposition in the hope that they could be an added help to the more earnest student. In some instances Sanskrit equivalents are also given.

Pronunciation

consonants
vowels

c = ch as in rich
a = u as in but
n = gn as in gnu
a = a as in art
t = th as in think
a = u as in fur
t = t as in to
i = i as in pin
d = th as in then
i = ee as in seen
m = ng as in ring
u = u as input
u = u as in rule

The vowels *e* and *o* are always long in Pali and Sanskrit, except when followed by a double consonant, e.g., *ettha*.

The aspirates *kh, gh, dh, th,* and *bh* are pronounced with the *h* sound immediately following, as in the English words, "blockhead," "pighead," "cathead," "loghead."

Foreword

It was with a great feeling of joy that I read the book on Buddhism written by Antony Fernando with Leonard Swidler. Writing a book on this topic, in English, and in an easily understandable style, is in itself something praiseworthy. But writing such a book expressly for Jews, Christians, and other Westerners, in an idiom that they can understand, is very opportune. It fills a void long lamented.

To write a book of this nature is not easy. Besides a thorough knowledge of the subject, great courage is necessary. For their courageous undertaking, the authors deserve the gratitude of Buddhists, Jews, and Christians alike.

The great interest that Westerners, and particularly Christians, are showing today in Buddhism is something about which I have firsthand knowledge. I have experienced it while being in charge of the Buddhist Mission in West Berlin. But I realized too, and with a certain sadness, that many interested non-Buddhists could not gain the familiarity with Buddhism that they desired, because of the shortage of suitable books. Most books on Buddhism available today were written primarily for practicing Buddhists living in Buddhist countries. They are not easily understandable by non-Buddhists belonging to a totally different cultural milieu. The Fernando-Swidler book, I feel, will be a very great help to Westerners trying to understand Buddhism and its message.

One feature that I particularly cherish in this book is the respect with which its authors treat Buddhism, Christianity, and Judaism. I have read exposés of Buddhism written by Christians whose hidden intention was to prove the superiority of Christianity. And I have read others by authors who think that Buddhism will be appreciated only by readers who hate Christianity. Neither of these two approaches really fits the modern world.

Typically, modern persons make their own judgments and decisions. They need only to be exposed to reality. They will then draw their own conclusions. The authors of this book understand this well. They respect the intelligence of their intended readers.

I am fully convinced that the revised edition of this book will help many Americans and other English-speaking readers come to know Buddhism in a way that will be truly beneficial to their lives. I wish the book every success.

ATURUGIRIYE SRI
GNANAWIMALA THERO
Satipattana Vipassana
Meditation Centre,
Aturgiriya, Sri Lanka
Buddhist Vihara, West Berlin

Toward Judeo-Christian-Buddhist Dialogue

Why a book on Buddhism for Christians and Jews? Because we have finally learned that we cannot "go it alone." For example, until the Second Vatican Council (1962-65) the Catholic Church had the reputation—deservedly so—of being resistant to dialogue. It had pretty well made its own the triumphalist statement of Pope Pius IX at Vatican I (1869-70): "*La tradizione son' io!—I am the tradition!*" (Bury, 124). But at Vatican II (1962-65) Catholicism did an about-face: "All the Catholic faithful" were mandated "to take an active and intelligent part in the work of ecumenism," for "the concern for restoring unity involves the whole Church, faithful and clergy alike. It extends to everyone" (*Unitatis Redintegratio*, nos. 4, 5 [Flannery, 465]). Catholics were to enter into theological dialogue with non-Catholics as equals, *par cum pari*, equal with equal.

During the course of Vatican II, Pope Paul VI issued his first encyclical (*Ecclesiam suam*, 1964) specifically on dialogue. He was not at all, in those early days, hesitant in his language:

"Dialogue is *demanded* nowadays. It is *demanded* by the dynamic course of action which is changing the face of modern society. It is *demanded* by the pluralism of society and by the maturity man has reached in this day and age. Be he religious or not, his secular education has enabled him to think and speak and conduct a dialogue with dignity" [quoted in *Humanae Personae Dignitatem*, no. 79 (Flannery, 1003)—emphases added].

Addressing itself beyond the borders of the Catholic Church, the Vatican Secretariat for Unbelievers recommended that "all Christians should do their best to promote dialogue... as a duty of fraternal charity suited to our progressive and adult age" (ibid.). A key notion in this interreligious dialogue and dialogue with nonbelievers is freedom for all parties concerned:

"Doctrinal dialogue should be initiated with courage and sincerity, with the greatest of freedom and with reverence.... If dialogue is to achieve its aims, it must obey the rules of truth and liberty. It needs sincere truth, thus excluding manipulated doctrinal discussion... in discussion the truth will prevail by no other means than by the truth itself. Therefore, the liberty of the participants must be ensured by law and reverence in practice" [ibid. (Flannery, 1010)].

To be sure, there is risk involved in dialogue: if one is really open to what other partners say, one has to reckon with the possibility that they will prove to be persuasive on some given issue. The Vatican has an incredibly strong statement supporting this position: "Doctrinal discussion requires perceptiveness, both in honestly setting out one's own opinion and in recognizing the truth everywhere, even if the truth demolishes one so that one is forced to reconsider one's own position, in theory and in practice, at least in part" (ibid.).

One must, then, ask: Why has this dramatic turn taken place in that highly conservative institution, the Catholic Church? (And one can effectively argue that if it has taken place there, then it can happen, if it has not already, in other less conservative religious traditions.) The answer to this simple question is quite complex, but I believe that a foundational element for the revolutionary turn is the deabsolutizing of the understanding of truth that has finally carried through in the Catholic Church—and other Christian and Jewish institutions. This is not the place to spell out that deabsolutizing process in detail.[1] But a few lines in its regard might be helpful.

Until the nineteenth century truth in the West was thought of in a very static manner: if something was found to be true in one place and time, then it was thought to be true in all times and places, and this was so not only in regard to statements about empirical data, but also about the meaning or morality of things. For example, if it was true for St. Paul to say that it was all right for slaves to be subject to their masters (in fact, he demanded it!), then it was always true.

But no Christian theologian today would admit the truth of the Pauline statement. In the past one hundred fifty years our understanding of truth statements in the West has become historical, perspectival, limited, interpretive—in a single word: relational. And that means deabsolutized. It is now understood that the particular historical circumstances within which a statement about the meaning of something arose have a profound influence on the statement—the very framing of the question, the thought categories in which it and the subsequent answers were expressed and developed, the kind of language used (poetic, mythic, scientific, legal), the audience for which it was intended, the goal it was meant to accomplish. Text can be properly understood only within *con*text; given a significantly new *con*text, a proportionately new *text* would be needed to convey the same meaning.

Further, what the new sense of history did to make time and circumstances dynamic elements in the new view of truth statements, the development of the sociology of knowledge did in regard to such things as class, status, and sex in society; these also had a profound effect on how one perceived and expressed reality. With the development of language analysis and hermeneutics (the "science of interpretation"), all our statements about the meaning of things were seen to be necessarily limited by the nature of language (although reality is multifaceted, we can speak of only one facet at a time: hence, all our truth statements are limited. And all such statements included an element of interpretation (*I* perceive reality, and *I* express *my* perception of it; although there clearly is an extramental *it*, I am inextricably bound up in the perception/ description of *it*).

By way of an example, an object (reality) is perceived, by a circle of perceivers. My perception/ description of the object (reality) may well be accurate, and therefore true, but it may not contain the perception/description of someone who is opposite me, which will also be true. An awareness of this nature of truth statements logically leads to the conclusion that I need to supplement my truth statements by being in dialogue with those who perceive reality other than I do. We shall never come to a complete perception/description of reality, but we can move toward an ever fuller one. Hence, dialogue and consequent self-transformation is dynamic, never-ending.

Dialogue is a conversation between persons with differing views, the primary purpose of which is for all participants to learn from the others so that they can change and grow in the perception and understanding of reality, and then act accordingly. Minimally, the very fact that I learn that my dialogue partner believes "this" rather than "that" proportionally changes my attitude toward that person, and a change in my attitude is a significant change in me. We enter into dialogue so that we can learn, change, and grow, not so that we can force change on the *other*, as one hopes to do in debate. On the other hand, because in dialogue *each* partner comes with the intention of learning and changing, one's partner in fact will also change. Thus, the goal of debate, and much more, is accomplished far more effectively by dialogue.

In addition, persons entering into interreligious dialogue must be at least minimally self-critical of both themselves and their own religious traditions. A lack of such self-criticism implies that one's own tradition already has all the correct answers. Such an attitude makes dialogue not only unnecessary, but even impossible, for we enter into dialogue primarily so that we can learn—which obviously is impossible if our tradition has never made a misstep, if it has all the right answers. To be sure, in interreligious dialogue one must stand within a religious tradition with integrity and conviction, but such integrity and conviction must include, not exclude, a healthy self-criticism. Without it there can be no dialogue—and, indeed, no integrity.

In interreligious dialogue there are at least three phases. In the first phase, we unlearn misinformation about each other and begin to know each other as we truly are. In phase two we begin to discern values in the partner's tradition and wish to appropriate them into our own tradition. If we are serious, persistent, and sensitive enough in dialogue, we may at times enter into phase three. Here we together begin to explore new areas of reality, of meaning and of truth, of which neither of us had even been aware before. We are brought face to face with this new, as yet unknown to us dimension of reality only because of questions, insights, and probings explored in dialogue.

There is something radically different about phases two and three, on the one hand, and phase one on the other. In the former we do not simply add on quantitatively another "truth" or value from the partner's tradition. Instead, as we assimilate it within our own religious self-understanding it will proportionately transform our self-understanding. Because our dialogue partner will be in a similar position, we shall then be able to witness authentically to those elements of deep value in our own tradition that our partner's tradition may well be able to assimilate with self-transforming profit.

All this of course will have to be done with complete integrity on each side, both partners remaining authentically true to the vital core of their own religious tradition. In significant ways that vital core will be perceived and experienced differently under the influence of dialogue, but if dialogue is carried on with both integrity and openness, the result will be that Jews will be authentically Jewish and Christians authentically Christian, not despite the fact that Judaism or Christianity has been profoundly "Buddhized," but because of it. And the same is true of a Judaized or Christianized Buddhism. There can be no room for syncretism here: Syncretism means amalgamating various elements of different religions into some kind of a (con)fused whole without concern for the integrity of the religions involved—which is not the case with authentic dialogue.

If we are to enter into dialogue with each other across religious lines, we shall have to learn to speak a language that will be understandable to our partner. The Jew and the Christian will have to learn something of the thought world, and language expressing it, of Buddhists, and Buddhists that of the Jews and Christians. This will be especially difficult inasmuch as the cultural milieux out of which the two perceptions/descriptions of reality arose are so very different, much more different than between Protestants and Catholics, or Christians and Jews, or even Jews or Christians and Muslims, for all these have a largely Semitic and biblical root.

In the West, Christianity and Judaism have been going through a deep crisis of demythologization. For modern critically-thinking Westerners the old language "from above" sounds too much like fairy tales; it is not convincing. The response of critically-thinking Christian and Jewish theologians has been to rethink their traditions with categories and language "from below...from within," that express the transcendent in terms of the immanent. It is precisely this language "from below," "from within," "immanent," humanity-based, that must be developed as interreligious dialogue moves beyond a bilateral basis, for that is the only kind of language that we can have in common. In terms of the Judeo-Christian-Buddhist dialogue it is humanity-based language that provides a most apt bridge between the Judeo-Christian and Buddhist traditions, not only because it is more and more the language of critically-thinking Jews and Christians, but also because it is likewise the language of much of Buddhism.

In terms of the conceptualization and expression of reality, much the same sort of misadventure overtook Judaism, Christianity, and Buddhism. All suffered the fate of an externalizing and ontologizing of the original, metaphorical, nonideological message of their founders. In this connection, the very names of the latter two religious traditions are revealing. The names come not from the *names* of the founding persons, Siddhartha Gautama and Jesus (Yeshua in Hebrew) of Nazareth, but rather from their *titles*: Buddha (Enlightened One) and Christ (Anointed One). Here already is reflected the move from the interior to the exterior. One need only compare the language that Jesus, Yeshua, uses to describe himself and his relationship to the ultimate source of reality, which he, in good Jewish—indeed, Pharisaic—fashion, calls Father, with the language of the great Christological councils of the fourth and fifth centuries to note clearly the move from metaphor to ontology. A similar comparison could be made of the language of Gautama in the Buddhist scriptures with some of the doctrines of later Mahayana Buddhism. Externalization and ontologization occurred in both instances.

What is necessary, then, in both traditions and in Judaism, is a *ressourcement*, a probing back to the sources, the original vital core, of each of the religious traditions, to the teachings embodied in both the words and lives of Yeshua and Gautama (there are of course immense historico-critical problems in achieving this goal, but significant progress has already been made), and the "rabbinical" founders of Judaism. When that is done one finds startlingly similar messages being taught by the original founders, despite the radically different milieux.

It will be worth our while to pause and look at a few of the teachings of Yeshua and the Rabbis (Yeshua too of course was a rabbi, but, for the sake of clarity, the term "rabbi" will not usually be used here of him) to see just how close they are to those of Gautama.

Gautama teaches that at the heart of the human experience of life there lies a basic dissatisfaction or suffering (*dukkha*); it is his goal to bring us to face *dukkha* and liberate ourselves from it. Ignorance of our lot is the cause of our slavery, and knowledge is the way to liberation. Yeshua's and the Rabbis' message too is one of liberation, a dialectic of slavery and liberation that comes about through truth. As a good teacher concerned for his disciples, Yeshua said to his Jewish followers: "If you follow my teaching you will be true disciples of mine, for you will know the truth, and the truth will set you free" (John 8:31-32).

Gautama rejected the idea that the true meaning of human life, salvation, was to be found first of all through religious rituals, the practice of asceticism, virtuous acts, or intellectual speculations — though some form of all these things have their proper place in human life—but in a deep interior wisdom that sets all things in their proper order. Fundamentally this is what Yeshua and the Rabbis taught with their central image, the reign of God. Unfortunately, Christians have often been misled by the usual

xvi

translation of the phrase *basileia tou theou*, as we have it in the New Testament Greek (Yeshua probably said *malkut shomaim* in Hebrew). In most instances, the phrase is translated as the "kingdom of God," as if Yeshua were speaking of a place, a realm. In fact, some of Yeshua's contemporaries made the same mistake and were corrected by him: "Some Pharisees asked Jesus when the *basileia tou theou* would come. His answer was: 'The *basileia tou theou* does not come in such a way as to be seen. No one will say, "Look, here it is!" or, "There it is!"; because the *basileia tou theou* is inside you (*entos hymon*)'" (Luke 17:20-21). Equally unfortunately, in Judaism a similar fate befell the Rabbis' image of *malkut shomaim*. The authentic meaning is that the reign of God is the situation wherein all things are rightly ordered according to their nature; God's will reigns.

Of course, the Rabbis and Yeshua spoke in theistic terms: God was the ultimate source and goal of reality, and so if things were ordered according to their nature, their fundamental structure, they would naturally be ordered according to the will, rule, reign of God. Gautama did not speak of God, either to affirm or deny; he was satisfied with speaking of a right ordering of things according to their ultimate authentic structure. Clearly there are differences here between the teachings of the Rabbis and Yeshua, on the one hand, and Gautama on the other, but there is an even more profound unity of their messages: our liberation is to be found within us in the right ordering of all things according to their fundamental structure.

In many different ways Yeshua and the Rabbis spoke of the reign of God, the interior right ordering of things, the importance of seeking it first, and its relationship to other values. At one point Yeshua said: "Rather, seek first of all the reign and its rightness (*dikaiosynen*), and all these things [he had been speaking of not worrying about what to eat or wear] shall be added to you" (Matt. 6:33). In the Talmud this saying of the Rabbis is recorded: "Did you ever in your life see an animal or a bird which had a trade? And they support themselves without trouble. And were they not created only to serve me? And I was created to serve my master.

Does it not follow that I shall be supported without trouble?" (*Kiddushin*, 4:14 [Smith, 137]). Yeshua and the Rabbis, like Gautama, did not reject the values of the body, but saw them as good things to be enjoyed within the right ordering of things. Then one can appreciate and enjoy all things for what they are, without any disordered clinging (*tanha* in the Pali of Gautama), but with a proper detachment, for as Yeshua said elsewhere: "Where your treasure is, there your heart will be also "(Matt. 6:21).

Just how focused the message of the Rabbis and Yeshua was on the interior right ordering of all things according to the structure of reality—and, in the theistic mode, that means on the source and goal of reality, God—can be seen in the summing up of the whole of religion in two great commandments: "You shall love the Lord your God with your whole heart (*kardia*) and with your whole soul (*psyche*) and with your whole understanding (*dianoia*). This is the great and first commandment" (Matt. 22:37-38). Here all the essential notions are interior ones: love, heart, soul, understanding. That is the first and great commandment; all others flow from it— the interior right ordering of all things. But in the Jewish tradition—and Yeshua was a very devout Jew—one does not live isolated like a hermit, and so Yeshua went on to make an *essential* link between that first commandment and the second, which he described as *like unto* the first (*homoia aute*): "The second is like unto it: You shall love your neighbor as yourself" (Matt. 22:39). Interior right ordering has immediate socio-ethical consequences. According to Yeshua, one does not "save" oneself alone, but liberation carries with it the impulse to share itself with others (as the medieval philosophers would say: *bonum sui diffusivum est*, goodness is diffusive of itself). This is exactly what the whole Buddhist tradition of the Bodhisattva is all about: the liberated ones teaching liberation to the unliberated.

It should be noted that in this summing up of religion in the two great commandments of love, Yeshua was not only quoting from the Hebrew Bible (Deut. 6:5 and Lev. 19:18), but was also following his Jewish predecessors in linking the two together as the sum of religion as expressed two hundred years earlier in *The*

Testaments of the Twelve Patriarchs. In fact, in Luke's version of the encounter between Yeshua and the Jewish expert in the law who asked about how to be "saved," it was the lawyer, not Yeshua, who summed up religion in the two great commandments of love; Yeshua simply agreed with him (Luke 10:25-28).

It is also important to discern that in the second commandment of love the Jewish tradition and Yeshua spoke of loving one's neighbor as one's self. There, indeed, is the standard, the authentic self, and there is the interior focus once again—which then has immediate outreach consequences. In another place Yeshua said: "But what does it profit a person to gain the whole world (*kosmon*) and suffer the loss of one's own self (*heauton*)?" (Luke 9:25). Should we humans not enjoy the cosmos? Yes, but we can really do so only through an interiorly rightly ordered self.

And in the sayings of Rabbi Nathan it is written: "To whomever saves a single soul [self] it is reckoned as if he saved the whole world.... To whomever destroys a single soul [self] it is reckoned as if he destroyed the whole world.... From this you learn that one human is worth the whole of creation" (*Aboth Rabbi Nathan*, 31 [Billerbeck, 1, 750]). It is the human self that follows the Torah— God's instruction on how to order life rightly—that is worth, and worthy of, the whole of creation.

One of the prime teachings of Gautama was that of concentration or focus of the mind—this is what the various techniques of meditation are aimed at. One should live fully in the "now." Of course, the fullness of "now" includes an awareness of the past and a looking forward to the future, but they both focus in on and move out from the present, which is to be embraced fully and consciously (the Western medieval motto was: *age quod agis*, "do what you are doing"). The same message is found in the words of Yeshua: "Therefore, do not worry about things for tomorrow; tomorrow will worry about itself. Sufficient for the day is the evil thereof" (Matt. 6:34).

In some of later Buddhism *nirvana* has come to mean something like the notion of heaven, a place where one goes to live happily after death. The same thing happened to *nirvana* that happened to the *basileia tou theou* and the *malkut shomaim*: it was reified and localized. In fact, to Gautama *nirvana* was very much like Yeshua's *basileia tou theou* and the Rabbis' *malkut shomaim*: a state of soul (*psyche*) wherein things are rightly ordered. *Nirvana* literally means "blown out." What is blown out? All of the false selves that most men and women mistake for their true, deep self. So deep is this true self according to Gautama that he refers to it as a "non-self," *anatta*, a non-self in the sense of what we have normally mistaken for our self. These pseudo-selves are "blown out" in nirvana, as is all *tanha*, "distorting craving," which is the source of the pseudo-selves. What is then left is the authentic self, at peace, deep peace, because it is rightly ordered in accordance with the structure of reality.

Yeshua spoke a different language, but sent much the same message, distinguishing authentic peace (his own) from pseudo-peace (that of the world). "Peace I leave you, my peace I give you, not as the world gives do I give you" (John 14:27). As a Palestinian Jew Jesus spoke not Greek but Hebrew and Aramaic. Thus, the word he used for peace was doubtless "*shalom*," which means much more than the mere cessation of exterior hostilities; it indicates an interior right ordering of all things that positively spreads out throughout the surrounding world. The Rabbis too had a similar message couched in Hebraic categories: "Peace (*shalom*) is great for it is set aside to' be the portion of the just.... Those who love the Torah have great peace (shalom).... Peace (*shalom*) is great for it will be granted to the gentle" (Billerbeck, 1, 216). Thus, for Yeshua and the Rabbis a synonym for *basileia tou theou/malkut shomaim*—and for *nirvana*—would have been the pregnant word "*shalom*."

In the end, those persons who attain liberation, salvation (which comes from the Latin word *salus*, "vibrant health"), who arrive at *nirvana*, at the *basileia/malkut*, at *shalom*, do not lead a grim, stoic life. Rather, only they are able to live life "to the hilt," for it is only they who, having things rightly ordered, can fully appreciate and enjoy them. Yeshua said as much in a stunning call to full life: "I have come that they may have life, and have it abundantly! "(John 10:10).

Let this suffice here to indicate something of the profound similarity of the messages of Gautama, Yeshua, and the Rabbis. Of course, there are also differences, but it must be asked whether these differences are over essentials or cultural variations, whether they are contradictory or complementary, whether they concern primary or secondary matters. In addition, there will be many more differences—and some similarities—when one moves into a comparative study of the religious traditions that flowed from Gautama, Yeshua, and the Rabbis over the millennia. That second move, of course, is important but, as in the very teachings of Gautama, the Rabbis, and Yeshua themselves, the right ordering of the original vital core of the religious tradition is primary; all other developments are to be seen in that light. Hence, our return to the sources, to the teachings of Gautama, the Torah, the Rabbis, and Yeshua.

Naturally such a *ressourcement* may not be done in a reductionist or primitivist manner, as if we were to "play" first-century Bible land or fifth-century B.C.E. India. Our contexts are different from that of the Rabbis, Yeshua, and Gautama, and therefore their messages must be applied to our contexts; we must make interpretations. And that is precisely where the history of the institutions comes in creatively: millions of other disciples of Gautama, the Rabbis, and Yeshua also tried to understand the teachings of their teachers and interpret them and apply them to their existential contexts. Their examples, their traditions, can be of immense help to us. But we must also be aware that these examples and traditions can be negative as well as positive ("the wise man learns by the mistakes of others; the fool by his own"). A tradition must always be tested by the original vital core in interpreting and applying it to the present.

Fortunately for us today the language of both the original vital core of Buddhism, Judaism, and Christianity (the teachings and lives of Gautama, the Rabbis, and Yeshua) and the language of modern critical thinkers (who are largely the ones interested in interreligious dialogue) are largely language "from below," "from within," the transcendent in the immanent—in short, humanity-based.

In this book Antony Fernando presents Buddhism in its original vital core in a language that is clear, "from within... from below," immanent, humanity-based. Connections are frequently made to the original vital core of the teaching of the Hebrew prophets, Yeshua, and the Rabbis with language that is likewise "from below... from within," immanent, humanity-based. Thus, the essential teachings of Buddhism appear as eminently meaningful, sensible, helpful to modern Westerners, whether Christians, Jews, or "nonreligious" humanists.

My contribution to this—the third—edition of this book has been to recast and expand the text so as to reach out to a broader readership: Jews, Westerners in general, Americans, women, and those concerned primarily with social justice.

LEONARD SWIDLER
Religion Department, Temple University
Philadelphia, Pennsylvania

Preface to the Revised Edition

When I first wrote the book *Buddhism and Christianity: Their Inner Affinity*, I intended it to be a handbook on Buddhism for Christians and particularly for Christians in my part of the world. Not in my wildest dreams did I suspect that it would be of use to any other group.

Dr. Leonard Swidler, editor and founder of the well-known *Journal of Ecumenical Studies* and a professor in the Department of Religion at Temple University, saw such a possibility after reading my book. Eventually he wrote to me asking if I would like to get the book published in the United States with some adaptations that would make it suitable for Jews and other Westerners also. He felt that such a book would help (as explained by him in the preceding statement) the Buddhist-Judeo-Christian dialogue. It was easy to see his point. As much as possible, interreligious dialogue has to be broadened, and so I agreed with his proposal.

This explains why the revised edition of my book bears a new title and why our names are both on the title page. I am grateful to Dr. Swidler for adapting my book to suit a larger and newer readership, but I am more grateful to him for the manner in which he has done it. Showing great ingenuity and sensitivity, he has adapted my book to its new purpose without in any way damaging or altering its content and message.

He has effected improvements in several areas of this book, the most important changes being in those sections that deal with Judaism. He has added a number of explanatory notes on Judaism that will help Jewish readers to understand Buddhism better and will aid them in comparing Buddhism with their own religion. These notes may not be very numerous or very extensive, and being interspersed in the text may not even be recognizable as coming from him, but they are of great value. They give a new face to the book, a face that Jewish readers will, it is hoped, feel at home with.

The fact that this book on Buddhism is now addressed to both Jews and Christians reduces in no way its applicability to Christians, the group for whom the first two editions were exclusively meant. On the contrary, a Christian using the book will now have the added advantage of learning more about Judaism.

Granted the fact that this is a book that is now addressed to both Jews and Christians, Dr. Swidler has taken the initiative to change the name Jesus to Yeshua in those chapters that treat of Judaism and Christianity together. Yeshua is undoubtedly the name that Jesus would have been known by among his contemporaries. That alteration by Swidler, controversial as it may appear to some traditional Christians, does have a value. It will remind Christians of Jesus' Jewish background, a fact of no little importance for readers of a book that compares Buddhism with both Judaism and Christianity.

The improvements effected by Dr. Swidler are not restricted to those areas connected with Judaism or with Christianity's Jewish background. To expand the audience of the book and to make it more accessible to Westerners, he has revised my English as well. In my earlier text I had not, for instance, been aware of sexism in our language. Often, I had used the word "he" in places where it could mean both "he" and "she," and "man" in places where it could mean both "man" and "woman." The alertness shown in matters such as this convinces me that Dr. Swidler has been sensitive to the feelings of all prospective readers of the book, including those who simply call themselves humanists.

Outside these additions and changes made by Dr. Swidler, I have made two major alterations in the second (Sri Lankan) edition of the book. I have considerably reduced that part of chapter 18 in which I had discussed at length the Christian notion of liberation. In an edition meant for Westerners, I thought the extensive treatment of such a topic would be superfluous. On the other hand, I have considerably enlarged the treatment in chapter 9 of the Buddhist notion of the "no-self." This is because the Buddhist "no-self" is a notion about which Westerners often seek greater clarification.

Except for such easily understandable changes effected by Dr. Swidler and myself, the text of my original book is reproduced here completely and without reduction or alteration.

I take this opportunity to thank Dr. Swidler for all that he has done to bring out my book in a revised edition adapted for a larger readership. In addition, I thank all those who have collaborated with him in this regard, especially the editors of Orbis Books. I cannot, of course, forget at this juncture the numerous persons who helped me bring out the earlier editions of the work. It would be too lengthy to mention all their names here. I want them to know, however, that I have not ceased to be grateful.

It is my sincere wish that this book, which is now a coproduct of Dr. Swidler and myself, will lead many Westerners to a deeper and more respectful understanding of Buddhism, and that it will also be instrumental in fostering the spirit of mutual understanding and friendship among Buddhists, Jews, Christians, and (religiously non-affiliated) humanists.

Introduction

A startling feature of the evolution of society in the last few decades is the extremely close contact that has developed between groups of very diverse cultural traditions. Not long ago, peoples of one culture lived quite self-assuredly in total aloofness from other cultures, ignoring at times their very existence. Even when their existence was acknowledged, it was generally maintained that no bridges of intercommunication could ever be built between those other cultures and their own.

With regard to the East-West division, for instance, it was Kipling who said, "East is East, and West is West, and never the twain shall meet." But the strange fact is that, quite contrary to such prognosis, the turn of events has been that the East and the West have not only met, but have also come to accept and respect each other. They have even started to live together in a spirit of mutual give and take.

This new development in intercultural relationships, particularly between the East and the West, has had a revolutionary effect on religion. For ages, religious persons feared communication in any form with persons of other religions. Religious authorities considered such inter-communication hazardous to the security of their own religions. But now intercommunication between religions has come to be an irreversible and irresistible factor of modern society. The resultant situation is such that new demands are being made on the study of religion itself.

In the field of religious education, a stage is beginning to evolve in which, at least at its higher levels, no study of one religion is complete without a parallel study of other religions. Higher religious education thus is progressively becoming a comparative study of religions and philosophies.

More than many other religionists, Christians—and now Jews too—are becoming alert to this new exigency, and are taking great pains to acquire as good a knowledge of other religions as possible. No major religion has been left out in the process. Nonetheless, the one among them that has succeeded in drawing the greatest attention is doubtless Buddhism. The reason probably lies in the fact that Buddhism is the only major contemporary religion that does not include within it the notion of God, a notion so central to Christianity and Judaism.

Unfortunately, however, for lack of adequate tools, many Christians and Jews are unable to satisfy their desire to explore Buddhism. This is not to say that there are no books on Buddhism. There are very good ones. But very few of them present Buddhism in comparison to Christianity—and certainly not in comparison to Judaism. Hardly any take into account the religious background of Christians and Jews, or the intellectual problems that Jews and Christians are bound to face when they venture upon such a study. Their thought patterns on religion have been molded from birth in such a way that a book on another religion that fails to take that frame of mind into account cannot fully answer their needs. This book represents an effort to fill that gap.

Buddhism, of course, like any other religion, cannot be dealt with comprehensively in one book. Buddhism has numerous aspects— history, philosophy, literature, art, architecture, and the like. Buddhism further, is a religion that has several denominations or sects. Each sect, be it the Theravada, or the different subsects of the Mahayana, has its own tradition and philosophy. All these sects can be studied both in their authentic forms and in their popular forms. To touch on all these aspects in a book such as this is impossible.

What I have tried to do here is to treat an aspect of Buddhism that any serious student of Buddhism must, sooner or later, examine— namely, the thought of Gautama, the Buddha. This I have tried to do by carefully elaborating the sermon that is accepted by all Buddhist groups as representative of the founder's thought and fundamental to Buddhism in all its forms: the sermon on the Four Noble Truths.

A serious study of this sermon alone is sufficient to give students an insight into all the Buddhist doctrines that they need to be acquainted with, such as *dukkha, samsara, nirvana, karma, paticca samuppada, anatta*. Some of these notions, being foreign to Christians, Jews, and other Westerners, are not easy to grasp. I have tried to explain them here in simple language, drawing parallels with Judaism and Christianity wherever possible. With the belief that it may be of help to beginners, I have at times used a few sketches by way of illustration.

With regard to the explanation of some of the above doctrines, I must make it clear that, basing myself on the sacred books of the Theravada tradition of Buddhism, I have not followed slavishly and in every detail the interpretations given to these doctrines in contemporary Theravada Buddhist manuals. This is because I feel convinced, as any student of the history of religions would be, that the contemporary interpretation of religious doctrines does not necessarily tally with what is said in the original sources. To be more authentic, one has to go back to the sources. A Christian of today, for example, will not be taken aback at such an approach. Scientific research on the Bible conducted in the last few decades has clearly shown how different the religion of Jesus is from interpretations subsequently dogmatized by different Christian denominations.

In this respect Buddhists, quite regrettably, are much behind Jews and Christians. Buddhist scholars are only beginning to realize, if at all, the importance and the urgency of such a going back to the roots. Nevertheless, scholars such as Venerable Buddhadasa Thera of Thailand, whom I have referred to in the course of this study and from whose writings I have derived much inspiration, could be said to have made a definitive start along this line. The writings of this monk, who is considered by many to be the leading Theravada thinker of our times, have become the object of serious scholarly investigation. The initiative of Venerable Buddhadasa, if pursued by others, is certain to bring about not only a deep reawakening in Buddhism itself, but also a greater appreciation of it by non-Buddhists. This is because such a return to the roots would help one see Buddhism in a much more coherent way than is permitted by contemporary manuals.

My main preoccupation here has been to show Gautama's doctrine of liberation in as coherent a way as possible and with the maximum fidelity to his original thought. Therefore, readers should not be surprised if they discover that some of the interpretations given here are not totally identical with the interpretations found in some contemporary Buddhist manuals.

Judging from its principal aim, this book could have been entitled "Buddhism: A Manual for Christians and Jews," for that is what it intends to be primarily. Such a title would have been very appropriate had I restricted my exposition to Buddhist liberation, and not gone on to add, in the last four chapters, reflections on the liberational aspects of Christianity and Judaism. I added those chapters because I felt that a Christian—and a Jewish—study of Buddhism had necessarily to end up as a comparative study. And so, anticipating a conclusion that such a study would lead to, I thought it more appropriate to entitle the first editions "Buddhism and Christianity: Their Inner Affinity." That of course does not mean that I am imposing that conclusion on the reader.

From my side, of course, I have no reason to hide that it is a conclusion that I had begun to adhere to firmly. Nor have I come to that conclusion arbitrarily or out of a syncretistic view of religions. My conclusion is the outcome of broadly based investigations into the two religions lasting over twenty years.

Without giving in to any feelings of undue self-consciousness, I have here to admit that I have been blessed with opportunities of acquainting myself with the two religions that one could consider a little out of the normal. First, purely from the academic side, I had a rare chance of studying the two religions up to a doctoral degree in each. Then from the side of practical acquaintance, I have had the privilege of living for respectably long periods in Christian seminaries and Buddhist monasteries. Finally, because teaching itself is a way to deeper learning, I have to say that I have also learned them as a teacher. I have taught both these religions at the graduate level.

But even with such opportunities it is not easy for one to come to a conclusion of inner affinity simply by contact with Christianity, Judaism, or Buddhism of any form. Christianity, Judaism, and Buddhism today, as is well known, are religions that do not have a uniform shape. They can be understood and practiced in diverse ways. Hoping that it will be of benefit to the reader in assessing the validity of my conclusions, I shall here include some paragraphs on my own life background and the forms of the two religions that came under my purview.

At a rather early stage in my life, prompted by my traditional Roman Catholic family back-ground, I had cherished a yearning to be a Christian missionary. To fulfill that yearning, already as a teenager, I joined a missionary society of the Roman Catholic Church. My membership in this society provided me with great opportunities to deepen my knowledge of Christianity. At one stage, I studied at the Faculty of Religious Education (*Institut Catéchétique*) of the *Institut Catholique*, Paris. The studies I did there made me see Christianity in a totally new light.

The Christian educators who lectured there were theologians conscientiously grappling with the problem of secularism. This was a time when Western secularism, and particularly rationalistic humanism, was challenging the most basic assumptions of Christianity, including the concept of God itself. To face this challenge, these theologians had no alternative but to go back to the Christianity of Jesus as portrayed in the Bible, and to re-present that Bible message in a language that the secular European of the day would understand. The religion of Jesus that they so presented had little to do with the ritualism, dogmatism, legalism, or institutionalism that later Christianity had often come to be associated with.

For them Christianity was first and foremost a path to salvation, a form of healing for the deepest human ills of individuals and society. Salvation, as they saw it, was not primarily a matter for dogmatic theorization. It pertained to the realm of experience, and particularly to an individual's inner struggle for growth and well-being. Religion was not something that one belonged to. It was something that one benefitted from. To me this root-form Christianity seemed very meaningful, and I began to cherish Christianity as I had never done before. It is in fact this Christianity of a liberational dimension that I have based myself on in my reflections given in the second part of this book.

It was after being exposed to this very challenging version of Christianity that I ventured on my study of Buddhism. I received my initiation to the subject at the *École des Hautes Études* Paris, and I followed it up with further study in two universities in Sri Lanka. In those places, I had the honor of having as my teachers some very renowned Buddhist scholars, both monks and lay persons. As an additional aid to study, at this time I resided mostly in Buddhist monasteries.

A decisive event in my search for the meaning of Buddhism was the contact I gained at this time (and quite casually at the start) with the radical Buddhist philosophy of Venerable Buddhadasa Thera of Thailand, to whom I have already made reference. He was a man grappling with the challenge of contemporary secularism in Asia, and he, in his turn, was resorting to Buddhism in its root form.

After coming in contact with the two religions in their root forms, quite naturally I began comparing them. What I thus compared were the teachings of Gautama and Jesus, the Jew, and not so much Buddhism and Christianity in their contemporary forms. The more I compared them, the more I saw an inner affinity between them. What Gautama and Jesus said may not have been fully identical. Each belonged to a different cultural background. But what they aimed at achieving was identical. Both had one human mission in view. Both wanted to bring a healing to the injured interior of human beings.

Such a comparative study necessarily had to have its effect on my original aspirations too. Once I saw an inner affinity in the mission of Gautama and Jesus, I began wondering whether Christians living in a Buddhist country, as I was, would be in conscience justified in identifying themselves with Christianity alone, or in being missionaries exclusively for Christianity.

Today I am strongly inclined to the view that those who want to be missionaries should do so for religion in general or, better, for religiousness as such, and not for this or that religion taken in a mutually exclusive sense. In the case of Buddhism and Christianity, one would have to be a missionary for both at the same time, for both have one common mission to fulfill in society. In the way I today see the inner affinity of these two religions, I personally have no difficulty at all in admitting that a person could be at one and the same time fully a Buddhist and fully a Christian, or even fully a Buddhist missionary and fully a Christian missionary.

My colleague in the preparation of the American edition of this book, Leonard Swidler, likewise was raised as a Roman Catholic, but in America in an environment that was not only Catholic, but also Protestant, Jewish: and humanist. His advanced studies and many years of university teaching and deep involvement in the ecumenical movement and interreligious dialogue, especially Jewish-Christian dialogue, have provided the resources to expand the scope of this American edition to make Judaism along with Christianity an equal partner in this comparative presentation of Buddhism.

Because of Leonard Swidler's and my background and experience, the conviction I have come to regarding the affinity between Buddhism, Judaism, and Christianity is a strong one, but one I have no right to force on the reader. Therefore, I have contented myself with allusions and indications of its likelihood, leaving readers to come to their own conclusions according to their own judgment.

But whether they agree with me or not in that second aspect of my book, I trust that the approach I have followed throughout will be of particular benefit to them as Jews and Christians in understanding and even appreciating Buddhism. To appreciate and respect anything good, wherever it is found, is, I trust, really a Jewish and a Christian—indeed, a human—virtue and obligation.

Finally, I should like Jewish, Christian, and other Western readers to see this exposition of Buddhism and the subsequent comparison of the three religions more as a meditative study than a speculative study. It is only through a meditative approach that a person will understand the message of any religious founder in its vital dimensions or liberational aspects. It is because I have wanted to leave it primarily as meditation that I have refrained from burdening the text with extensive footnotes and references. To an intelligent Christian and Jew engaged in meditation, the words of Gautama, Jesus, the Hebrew Bible, and the Rabbis are by themselves enough.

PART ONE

HUMAN LIBERATION ACCORDING TO GAUTAMA

Chapter One

Life and Personality of Gautama

The best introduction to the philosophy of great persons is their own life, for events in persons' lives are generally connected with developments in their thought. This is not less true of Gautama and his philosophy.

Unfortunately for us, we know only very little of Gautama's own life. He lived twenty-five hundred years ago, or five hundred years before Jesus, and the little we know of him from the scriptures may not be historical in every detail. Certain facts contained in the scriptures seem to have been intentionally fitted in by redactors to bring out the particular role he played as the founder of Buddhism.

Such uncertainty in biographical details is not a weakness peculiar to the Buddhist scriptures. As any Bible student today knows only too well, we cannot build up a strictly historical account of Moses' life from the Hebrew Bible or of Jesus' life from the gospel narratives themselves. The evangelists, for example, were not preoccupied, as we are today, with the need for recording a diary account of Jesus' life and activity. They narrate events of his life only as necessary for their purpose, which was religious instruction. Thus, what the Gospels have preserved for us are educational rather than historical accounts of the life of Jesus. The same can be said of Moses and the Rabbis in the Talmud.

Gautama's life story seems to be arranged with a similar purpose— namely, to make his teaching more acceptable and more meaningful. As far as we are concerned, that does not matter, because thereby his biography becomes a kind of commentary on his teaching. The scriptural account of Gautama's life, therefore, is worthy of serious study.

Home Life

To begin with, it is useful to keep in mind that the term "Buddha" is an honorary title attributed to him, very much like "Israel" given to Jacob or the name "Christ" given to Jesus. His family name was Gautama, his personal name Siddharta. Like the title "Christ" (Messiah), the title "Buddha" was known to the people long before Gautama Siddharta was born.

The term "Buddha" literally means "enlightened" or "mentally awakened"; "Christ" means "anointed" or "sent by God"; and "Israel" most probably means "let God rule." These three honorary titles designate the function and the mission each of these religious founders fulfilled (Jacob was the founder of the nation of Israel). The significance of these three terms is such that a correct understanding of their definitions alone could show what characteristically differentiates Buddhism from Judaism and Christianity. According to Buddhism, one becomes a great person or a liberated person when one's mind (by the power that is within it) becomes enlightened enough to look at life realistically. According to Judaism and Christianity, one is a great person or a saved person insofar as one is in right relationship with God. It is this that makes such persons lead their life realistically.

The terms "Buddha" (and Buddhism), "Christ" (and Christianity), and "Israel" (and Israelite religion, which later developed into Judaism, named after Judah, one of the twelve sons of Jacob—i.e., Israel) thus ultimately represent two approaches to human nobility and perfection—the Buddhist and the Judeo-Christian. One view of perfection starts with God and goes to humanity (which, of course, is true both of Judaism and its offspring, Christianity), the other starts and stops with humanity itself. The background of Gautama's life helps us to better understand the reason behind his particular approach.

Gautama Siddharta was born in a materially well-to-do family. His father was chief of a clan called the Sakyans, on the Nepalese frontier, in a region called Kapilavastu. There were many such chiefs in the same kingdom. His mother, Mahamaya, was princess of the Kolian clan.

The fact that the father of Gautama was a civic chief is important. It means that Gautama belonged not to the Brahmin or the priestly caste, but to the Kshatriya or the soldier caste. Had he belonged by birth to the Brahmin caste, traditionally preoccupied with rites and rituals, gods and goddesses, it would not have been easy for him to found a religion in which the god-concept would have been absent.

The birth of Gautama took place outside his home, while his mother was on a journey. She was on her way from Kapilavastu to her parental home in Devadaha. In India, a woman goes to her mother for the delivery of the first baby, which probably is the reason for the journey Mahamaya had undertaken. Gautama Siddharta was born in the park of Lumbini under the shade of a sal tree. According to a virgin-birth legend found in certain books of the Mahayana tradition, Gautama came into the world from the side of his mother, without causing her any pain, while she was holding a branch of the tree. Mahamaya died on the seventh day, so Gautama missed the tender care of a mother. He was reared by his mother's sister, Prajapati Gotami.

His education, in keeping with the family traditions of the Kshatriya or soldier caste, was necessarily a very good one. Like all other noblemen, he would have been well trained in archery and the art of war.

Marriage in India is an event that is woven into an intricate tradition. At times, partnerships are decided by parents soon after the birth of the child or in early childhood. We do not know anything about the background of Gautama's marriage except that he married his cousin Yasodhara at the age of sixteen. She was the only daughter of King Suppabuddha.

Renunciation

Gautama's father had great plans for his son: he wished for him a glamorous political career. To encourage him toward such a goal, he tried to provide his son with many luxuries. It is said that he took special precautions to keep the miseries of life from his son's inquiring eyes. His efforts were not successful, for reality can never escape a person who is alert. Gautama did see the reality of life, and his sight or insight was powerful enough to bring an altogether new turn into his life.

Gautama's understanding of the reality of life, which was the prelude to his first major decision about his career, is traditionally presented as four visions:

1. a man weakened with age,
2. a sick man with infested skin and bones,
3. a dead man being taken into the cemetery,
4. a recluse with a calm and serene face.

Of these four scenes, the first three fall into one category and the fourth into another. The first three show facets of the reality of *ailing humanity*. The last shows one possible *relief* from it.

These four visions, if rightly understood, could give us a correct insight into the doctrine that he later taught. He taught a way of escaping the suffering caused by old age, sickness, and death. The way is the life of renunciation. Of course, as everybody knows, even a monk who renounces the world does not escape sickness, old age, and death. But he does escape the agony caused by them inasmuch as his mind is not unduly attached to transient aspects of life, and he does not consider them to be ultimate values.

This shocking discovery of the transitoriness of life, and the subsequent folly of being attracted by transitory values, caused Gautama to decide to renounce the world and become an ascetic. He was twenty-nine years of age when he took this step. He was no longer a teenager, having behind him already thirteen years of married life. The decision taken at such an age must be viewed as well-considered and mature.

A Christian or Jewish student may be somewhat shocked at the idea of a married person leaving his wife and child behind to enter the monastic life. We must view such happenings in the light of the social traditions prevalent at the time. Leaving home for the practice of asceticism after a period of married life was an approved form of behavior in Hindu society. According to the Hindu ideal, a person aspiring to perfection had to organize his life in a certain gradation. He had first to be a celibate student, then a married man, and finally either an ascetic or a hermit. According to that commonly accepted tradition, Gautama's behavior was not at all abnormal. Further, if the Indian family system is taken into account, where a strong sense of unity prevails among relatives, leaving behind a wife and child did not amount to an abandonment. They were always taken care of by the parents, parents-in-law, or uncles and aunts.

Even though he renounced family life in keeping with an existing tradition, what is important for us to realize is that he did not follow that tradition blindly. That is where the particular greatness of Gautama's decision lies. He was bold enough to challenge the notion of renunciation and of religion itself. He was sharp enough to suspect that, just as much as life in the world, life as a hermit or an ascetic too could itself be a trap. That is why the scriptures do not say that he left home just to become an ascetic or a monk. According to the Buddhist scriptures, he left family life "in quest of the supreme security from bondage, in quest of *Nibbana*" (MN, I, 163, Sutta 26).

Search

His first experiment was with systems of meditation. He placed himself under the guidance of two well-known yogi teachers of the time, Alara-Kalama and Uddaka Ramaputta. It is very likely that Gautama profited from this training in yoga, and that he acquired from his teachers a facility in meditation. But Gautama did not attach an all-exclusive importance to the techniques of yoga, nor did he look approvingly at the preoccupation of these yogi teachers with the meditational states known as trances.

Meditation, to be sure, is a very important feature in Buddhism, but Gautama was not interested in meditation simply for the sake of meditation. For Gautama, the right type of meditation had to lead an individual not just to an ephemeral experience but to an *insight* into the deeper realities of life. The type of meditation he later undertook to promote (as we shall see in chap. 14, below) is a system of meditation called Insight Meditation (*vipassana bhavana*).

The second stage of his search consisted of an experiment with asceticism. After leaving the yogi teachers Gautama joined a monastery or ashram in which five ascetics lived together. Such ashrams were common in the India of Gautama's day. This particular monastery was situated in Uruvela by the river Neranjara at Gaya. The names of the five ascetics, as preserved for us in the scriptures, are Kondanna, Bhaddiya, Vappa, Mahanama, and Assaji.

These monks practiced the strictest asceticism. They believed that self-mortification and self-torture had in themselves a liberative power. Even in modern India it is not uncommon to find ascetics and even lay persons who believe in that philosophy. At certain penitential shrines, penitents can be seen sticking themselves with hooks, cutting themselves with blades and spikes, rolling on hot sand, walking on nailed shoes, and the like.

These monks believed mainly in fasts, living exclusively on leaves and roots. Gautama followed those disciplines so rigorously that the absolute paucity of nourishment left him a physical wreck. Describing the emaciated state of his body that resulted therefrom, he said: "Rigorous have I been in my ascetical discipline. Rigorous have I been beyond all others. Like wasted, withered reeds became all my limbs" (MN, I, 246, Sutta 36).

6

It was not long before he realized the utter futility of such self-mortification to achieve liberation. He soon saw that what is required for liberation is not self-mortification but self-discipline or self-mastery. As soon as he discovered that pure asceticism could not give the deeper form of mental liberation he sought after, he bade his companions good-bye and began to pursue his search all by himself.

The period of search under yogi teachers and with ascetics is mentioned in the scriptures as having lasted six years. There are two important facts about Gautama's life and doctrine that stand out very strikingly from this period of his search.

First, it shows, without any doubt, that Gautama had a very strong spirit of determination. Six years is a long period and any ordinary person would have given up or been satisfied with an easier solution. Gautama had extraordinary determination. He was also very sincere in whatever he did. Be it meditation or asceticism, he practiced with the full devotion of his heart and soul. All that indicates clearly that he had a mind of his own. He did not accept tradition or authority without judgment and so was able to disagree with traditions and teachers.

Secondly, this period of experimentation shows a clear evolution of his convictions. A very clear element of his philosophy is the uncompromising rejection of asceticism. His system was called a "middle path" primarily because he wanted to declare himself against asceticism in its physical and external form. He considered such asceticism just as harmful to human perfection as is self-indulgence.

After leaving the ascetical school, Gautama continued his search, reflecting on liberation and the path to it in total solitude. Under a large shady tree, which eventually came to be called the "Bodhi tree" (in short "Bo tree" and literally, the "tree of enlightenment" or "wisdom") he meditated on his past life and on the differing states of the unliberated lives of others. He sought the reasons that keep men and women in an unliberated state and there he discovered the real nature of human suffering, the cause of it, the possibility of escape from it, and the path for such an escape. It is this discovery that is referred to by the technical term "enlightenment," *Bodhi*. He saw the reality of human suffering and the possibility of human joy in a way that he had never seen before. His conviction was such that he realized, once and for all, the true joy of existence. The conviction was so powerful that with it he felt a sense of mission to preach it to the whole world. A Jew or a Christian would have expressed this experience, in the language proper to them, as "revelation." But for Gautama it was something that "arose" in him by itself as a result of his own concentration.

He expressed this experience of "enlightenment" in a spirit of joy and humility:

Being myself subject to birth, aging, disease, death, sorrow, and defilement, seeing danger in what is subject to these things, seeking the unborn, unaging, diseaseless, deathless, sorrowless, undefiled, supreme security from bondage—*Nirvana*—I attained it. Knowledge and vision arose in me. Unshakable is my deliverance of mind [MN, I, 166, Sutta 261.

Gautama was so enraptured by his discovery that he is said to have spent seven weeks in meditation in the same area before starting out to fulfil his new mission. The second of these seven weeks he is said to have spent looking with immense gratitude at the tree that shaded him. This shows the magnitude of his sense of discovery. Though in an entirely different field, the "eureka" feeling that he experienced could not have differed from the feeling that in a later era Isaac Newton experienced when he discovered gravity, or Pasteur, germs, or Columbus, America.

Mission

Gautama started his preaching mission with those he had known before. The first group he approached were the five ascetics with whom he had lived. His sense of friendship was such that he did not reject them as individuals, even though he rejected their philosophy. He wanted to share with them his newly-won insight into liberation and traveled one hundred fifty miles to meet them. When he first spoke to them, they did not attach any importance to his views but, like any great person, Gautama knew how to convert them to him by the very simplicity of his approach. When their opposition to him was at its highest, he simply asked them: "Have I ever spoken to you like this before, as one who claims to know the truth?" This simple appeal appeared irresistible to them. When they were ready to listen, he started his exposition of his new system of liberation, which he termed the Middle Path:

> These two extremes, monks, are not to be approached by him who has withdrawn from the world. Which two? One is that which is linked and connected with lust, through sensuous pleasures, because it is low, of the uncultured, of the mediocre man, ignoble and profitless. The other is that which is connected with mortification and asceticism because it is painful, ignoble, and incapable of achieving the target. Avoiding both these extremes, monks take the Middle Path which is the Eightfold Path, namely, right view, right thought, right speech, right action, right livelihood, right effort, right mindfulness, right meditation. It is this which brings insight, brings knowledge and leads to tranquility, to highest awareness, to full enlightenment, to *Nirvana* [VP/MV, 10, i, 6:171].

This extract is the preface to the most important philosophical exposition of Gautama: the sermon of the Middle Path. It is also called the sermon on the Four Noble Truths, for in it he develops, in the form of four truths, the reasons that make his path the most suitable path to liberation.

These five monks became his first followers and the first members of the monastic order that he established. Soon afterward, the *Vinaya Pitaka* says, a group of fifty-five young lay persons joined the order. Many others followed suit and the order grew very rapidly.

The monastic order that Gautama established has a very special place among all the monastic orders that the world has known. Gautama's monastic order, in its earliest form, was probably the only order in the history of humanity that had no rite, ritual, or sacrifice. It probably would have been also the least ascetic of all the orders that the world had known because it rejected the very principle that asceticism has a liberative value.

Gautama established a monastic order for women as well. But admission into the orders of the monks or the nuns was not the only way of gaining discipleship under Gautama. Lay persons too were accepted as disciples.

Quite regrettably, this is an aspect that has been left unstressed in the Theravada tradition. The sermon called the *Maha Vaccagotta Sutta* indicates that a large *lay* discipleship consisting of men and women, married as well as unmarried, formed as great a part of Gautama's organization as did monks and nuns (MN, I, 490-91). Gautama clearly affirmed that full liberation was also within their reach.

One of the special functions of the monk was that of preaching the doctrine. Buddhism from the beginning was missionary in outlook. The formula Gautama used in sending out the first group of missionaries shows clearly the nature and aim of Buddhist missionary work.

> Delivered am I, monks, from all forms of enslavement. You also are delivered. Go now, and wander for the welfare and happiness of the many, out of compassion for the world, for the gain, welfare, and happiness of the entire

10

universe. Let not two of you proceed in the same direction. Proclaim the *dhamma* [doctrine] that is so excellent, so meaningful and so perfect. Proclaim the life of purity, the holy life, consummate and pure. There are beings with a little dust in their eyes who will be lost through not learning the *dhamma*. There are beings who will understand dhamma [VP/MV, 21,I,11].

The missionary activity of the order was crowned with great success in Gautama's own time. The secret of success was simply the relevance of the doctrine he preached; at a time when ideas of religion and liberation were so confused, he presented a purified view of religion and liberation that was easy to understand and precise enough to follow. The nobility of his family background could also have been a contributive factor. There were many kings, rulers, and wealthy men who gave him generous support.

This, of course, does not mean that Gautama did not have his own problems and setbacks. One of his greatest sufferings could well have been the opposition to his leadership in the order that was fostered by a monk who was also a cousin, Venerable Devadatta. The latter struggled very hard to take over the leadership of the order. The difficulties that Gautama experienced in such matters were so great that at times he went into long retreats in the forest to escape from them. It is difficult to say whether he succeeded or not in solving all the rifts that were beginning to take place within the order. All we know from history is that soon after his death the order divided into different groups. In spite of that division, the basic message of Gautama has been preserved by all the groups.

We cannot conclude the story of this great religious leader without a word concerning his personal sanctity. According to Gautama there were four basic qualities that were to characterize any Buddhist saint or liberated person. They are:

1. *metta*-friendliness or loving kindness
2. *karuna*-compassion

3. *mudita*-gentleness
4. *upekkha*-equanimity.

These four qualities that he recommended to others were also qualities that he practiced himself. One little incident shows how seriously he practiced such virtues in his own life. As the order grew and established itself in distant places, he made it a point to visit groups of monks residing in different areas and assure himself of their welfare. One monastery he so visited had a monk who was very ill. The monk was suffering from an advanced skin disease. The eczema had spread so much that his entire body seemed one single sore. Blood and pus oozed out to the extent that his clothes were stuck to his body. His companions, because of the filthiness of his state, had kept aloof and abandoned him to endure his misfortune alone.

Gautama visited this monk in the company of his close associate, Ananda. Then, taking a basin of water and a towel, Gautama washed the patient himself and cleaned him. After doing whatever was possible to bring relief to him, he walked down to the little huts of the other monks. He inquired from them about the sick monk and why they neglected to look after him. Their reply was that, inasmuch as he was certain to die, he was of no benefit to the order. Then, with the intention of opening their eyes to the heartlessness of such behavior, Gautama said:

> Monks, you do not have a mother, you do not have a father here who can tend you; if you, monks, do not tend one another, who is there to tend you? Remember that whoever tends a sick person, as it were, tends me [VP/MV, 302, viii, 26:3].

Gautama thus showed himself to be a person, who practiced the virtues he preached.

Gautama lived to the age of eighty. His death occurred at Kusinara, one hundred twenty miles from Benares, in what is now Uttara Pradesh. The last words he addressed to his assembled disciples are very significant:

> *Vayadhamma samkhara,*
> *appamadena sampadetha*
>
> (Life is transient.Strive ahead
> with attentiveness.)

Thus, the need for effort and for attentiveness to reality was stressed during his last moment on earth, as it had been throughout his life.

Even though his life ended twenty-five hundred years ago, his message continues to live on even in our day. Buddhism is found in Sri Lanka, Thailand, Cambodia, Laos, Vietnam, Nepal, Tibet, China, Japan, Korea, Mongolia, Taiwan, and in some parts of India, Pakistan, and Malaysia. There are many in the West too who today adhere to his teaching. That wide diffusion shows that his message is a challenge to modern women and men, as it had been to those of his day.

It would be no exaggeration to add that it is also a challenge to the modern Christian and Jew, especially those living in a Buddhist environment. Unfortunately, it has happened that Christians coming from the West have, in the past, tried to diffuse Christianity without giving any thought at all to the richness of Gautama's message alive in those lands. Even if, due to ambiguous historical circumstances peculiar to those centuries, their behavior would be pardonable, Christians—and Jews—of today living in a Buddhist country can no longer be excused if they do not try at least to investigate Gautama's message and see how it compares with their own beliefs.

Chapter Two

The Sermon on the Four Noble Truths: Exposition of the Middle Path

The sermon of the Four Noble Truths is the best and safest text for attempting to understand the philosophy of Gautama. It is Gautama's very first sermon, and the one that is universally accepted as the clearest summary of all that he taught and stood for.

It is this text that will form the core of our investigation in this book. It is therefore only appropriate that the full text be given at the start. In the *Vinaya Pitaka* it reads as follows:

> (a) Two extremes, monks, are not to be approached by him who has withdrawn from the world. Which two? One is that which is linked and connected with lust, through sensuous pleasures, because it is low, of the uncultured, of the mediocre man, ignoble and profitless. The other is that which is connected with mortification and asceticism, because it is painful, ignoble, incapable of achieving the target. Avoiding both these extremes, monks, take the Middle Path,... which brings insight, brings knowledge, and leads to tranquility, to full knowledge, to full enlightenment, to *Nirvana*.
>
> And monks, what is this Middle Path that leads to *Nirvana*? It is indeed, the Noble Eightfold Path, namely right understanding, right thought, right speech, right action, right livelihood, right effort,

right mindfulness, right concentration. The Middle Path leads to *Nirvana*.

(b) Now monks, this is the Noble Truth as to sorrow. Birth (earthly existence) indeed is sorrowful. Disease, death, union with the unpleasing, separation from the pleasing is sorrowful; in brief, desirous transient individuality (five grasping aggregates) is sorrowful.

Again, monks, this is the Noble Truth as to the origin of sorrow. It is the recurring greed, associated with enjoyment and desire and seeking pleasure everywhere, which is the cause of this sorrow. In other words, it is the greed for sense-pleasure, greed for individual existence, and the greed for non-existence.

Again, monks, this is the Noble Truth as to the cessation of sorrow... the complete cessation, giving up, abandoning, release and detachment from greed.

And this once more, monks, is the Noble Truth as to the path to the cessation of sorrow. It is indeed that Noble Eightfold Path: right understanding, right thought, right speech, right action, right livelihood, right effort, right mindfulness, right concentration. The Middle Path, monks, leads to *Nirvana*.

(c) As soon, monks, as my knowledge and sight concerning these four Noble Truths became complete, I knew that I had attained supreme and full enlightenment. I became aware and fully convinced that my mind was liberated, that existence in its unhappy form had ended, that there would no longer be an unhappy survival.

Thus, spoke the Blessed One. The five monks, rejoicing, welcomed the word of the Blessed One [VP/MV, 10, i, 6:17-23].

Theme of the Sermon

Such is the text of the sermon as found preserved for us in the oldest Buddhist manuscripts. The English translation given here is made from the Buddhist scriptures written down in the Pali language. Pali and Sanskrit are the languages in which the Buddhist scriptures in their oldest forms have come down to us.

Even though this is probably the most important sermon of Gautama, it is very unlikely that a reader will find its message self-evident. Buddhists who have been acquainted with it from their earliest days, and have learned it by heart in the original Pali, may of course feel differently. But a person from another religious background will almost certainly be at a loss to find the sequence of ideas in it, or the link between its different sentences and paragraphs.

This is due to no fault of the reader, or even of the text. Ancient texts in any field of knowledge hardly ever enjoy the easy discernibility of modern writings. This text records a sermon, or the essence of a sermon, preached twenty-five hundred years ago. Though it may not be immediately evident, this sermon has just one central theme developed in three sections.

Section a. The two initial paragraphs could be considered an introduction. It spotlights the main purpose of the sermon. Gautama wanted by this sermon to present a new religious code, or "path." He described it by enumerating the eight ingredients or items that constitute it. Naming it accordingly, he called it the "Eightfold Path." The eight words (or sixteen, if we also include the adjective "right," which precedes each term) sum up a whole new religion.

But for a special reason that was in his mind and that we shall discover eventually, he called this Eightfold Path a Middle Path. According to his own explanation, this new path is situated between the two extremes of loose sensuality and rigid asceticism.

Section b. The second part, which is generally considered to be the central part of the sermon, contains four assertions termed "Noble Truths" (paragraphs 3, 4, 5, 6). Through them he proves systematically and logically that the Eightfold or Middle Path is the most appropriate way of religion for human beings. Through them he tries to establish the fact that, even though his path may not contain all the traditional elements of religion, it is a path that is complete by itself.

The basis for his argument is a simple one. For him only those elements should form part of religion that are intrinsic to its chief function. The chief function of religion is the liberation of human beings from their inner suffering. Any elements that do not serve that purpose are useless. The Eightfold Path contains all that is necessary to heal human beings from their inner suffering.

Section c. The third part of the sermon is contained in the penultimate paragraph. In it he points to his own personal experience as an additional argument for the validity of the Eightfold Path. He says that in his own case the Eightfold Path worked wonderfully and yielded all the desired results. The practice of the Middle Path brought him to a life of peace and happiness that he had never enjoyed earlier.

That is a brief synthesis of the sermon of the Four Noble Truths. But of course, it has to be investigated in greater detail if its message is to be discovered in all its comprehensiveness and complexity.

Revolutionary Dimensions of the Middle Path

Something must be said about the significance of the term "Middle Path" if we are not to bypass the intrinsic novelty of its content. The term "Middle Path" as used in our contemporary everyday language is a very soft-sounding term suggesting compromise. It has nothing aggressive or revolutionary about it. In fact, what it insinuates is that the revolutionary elements accompanying the movements of the extreme left or extreme right are not contained in it. But we must be careful not to think of Gautama's Middle Path in the same way. Of course, it is not impossible that Gautama himself intended this term as a kind of shock absorber to lessen the fears that could arise about the revolutionary nature of his philosophy. Great men and women believe in a revolution of action rather than of words.

Whatever it be, a little close inspection is enough to show that a more revolutionary philosophy of religion than that of Gautama had hardly been presented by anyone before. The originality of his philosophy is such that by it he challenged a number of religious traditions considered sacred and unchallengeable for centuries. To see that aspect of his sermon we must take into consideration the context in which he preached it, and particularly the audience to which it was addressed.

Gautama presented this sermon to a group of five ascetics whom he had known very well. He had lived with them for nearly six years and experimented with their form of religious life. They were a group for whom sanctity consisted of regular fasts, religious penances, and as much aloofness from society as possible. While in their company he had followed their philosophy ungrudgingly and with great zeal.

He lived on leaves and roots and on a steadily reduced pittance of food. As his garb, he wore rags collected from rubbish heaps. He slept in cemeteries among corpses and at times on beds of thorns. He followed their ascetical code until he found himself a physical wreck.

Quite naturally he judged such a philosophy incompatible with his religious aspirations and of no avail to his goals in life. He parted company with his fellow ascetics. But now, after his experience of religious enlightenment, it was to them he returned to propound his own newly developed philosophy. What he had to present was a non-ascetical and even anti-ascetical philosophy. It was this philosophy that he introduced as a middle path that avoided the two extremes of sensuality and asceticism.

With regard to the first extreme, what Gautama says is nothing unusual. There is nothing new in the idea that a religious person should avoid a life of sensuality. No laborious arguments are necessary to prove the unsuitability of such an extreme as a religious path. No one, and least of all his ascetical audience, would have challenged that. But his objection to asceticism as a way of religion is very different. Asceticism has from time immemorial been a tradition-sanctioned, society-approved way to religious liberation. The popular belief even today is that greater asceticism implies greater holiness.

The challenge of the philosophy of Gautama is exactly there. He regards asceticism as something extrinsic to the purpose of religion and so left no place for it in the Eightfold Path. The revolution in religious ideas that he initiated thereby is not a small one.

Of course, one could ask why Gautama, who so firmly rejected asceticism, advocated a form of monasticism. The answer is simple. First of all, monasticism is not asceticism. Monasticism is only a form of separation from family life, and not necessarily a life of self-torture. Secondly, even though he was a monk and the founder of a monastic order, he did not restrict his discipleship to monks. Lay persons too were among his full-fledged disciples. But what is still more important for us to note is that the type of monasticism he advocated was the most liberal and the least ascetical of all the monastic systems that history had known until then.

It is unfortunate, however, that contemporary Buddhist monasticism does not represent adequately the philosophy of the Middle Path in its original form. Buddhism today (like all religions of modern times for that matter) attaches an undue importance to the externals of religion.

For Gautama religion, as well as monasticism, was something primarily of the mind. This is probably best illustrated in his attitude toward the attire of monks. The latitude he gave his monks in the choice of garb will, particularly to a traditionalist, appear astounding.

Today monks are distinguished from lay persons by the saffron robe they wear. In Gautama's day, most non-Buddhist ascetics also wore saffron-colored robes. But from many early Buddhist texts and particularly the *Vinaya Pitaka* it is absolutely certain that the Buddha was indifferent to the dress of his monks. Contrary to tradition, he clearly approved the use of even lay garments by monks, leaving the option of wearing religious habit or lay clothing to the individual monk.

He was indifferent to his own dress and there are clear indications that at times he wore lay garments. According to the *Vinaya Pitaka*, on one occasion, when a devoted benefactor offered him a silk garment meant for a lay person, he accepted it and announced to the monks:

> I allow you, monks, the use of lay garments. He who wishes may use monastic garments. He who wishes may use lay garments. But with either, what I commend is the spirit of contentment [VP/MV, 280, viii, 1:35].

In later Theravada commentaries and particularly the *Samantapasadika*, the chief commentary on the *Vinaya*, composed seven to eight centuries later, this permission was construed to suit the rigorous practices prevailing at the time. "Lay garments" were interpreted as garments given by lay persons with the expectation that they would be dyed saffron before being worn. But such a forced explanation does not do justice to either Gautama's Middle-Path philosophy or to the original scriptural texts.

The anti-ascetical attitude of Gautama, of which this latitude regarding monastic garb is one example, is not the only thing that is revolutionary in the philosophy of the Middle Path. There are many other revolutionary elements contained in it. His disregard for rites and ritual, as also for the worship of gods and goddesses, are two others.

Thus from numerous angles it is very clear that his Middle-Path religion is more revolutionary than would appear at first sight. We should also not think that he presented his new stand on religion haphazardly or arbitrarily. He provided justification for it through what is called the Four Noble Truths. It is this that we now have to analyze in greater detail.

Chapter Three

Universality of Human Sorrow: First Noble Truth

According to Gautama, religion was a cure. The *raison d'être* of its existence, its most primary function, was to bring healing to persons suffering from a particular type of internal ailment. Inasmuch as Gautama's aim in his first sermon was to clarify what religion was and what it had to be, he began by expounding very precisely what the ailment was for which religion was to provide a cure. In the First Noble Truth itself, he named it. It was "suffering" or "sorrowfulness," in the sense of being full of sorrow (the word in Pali is *dukkha*):

> Now, monks, this is the Noble Truth as to sorrow. Earthly existence itself is sorrowful. Decay is sorrowful. Disease, death, union with the unpleasing, separation from the pleasing is sorrowful; the wish which cannot be fulfilled is sorrowful; in brief, the desirous, transient individuality is sorrowful [VP/MV, 10, i, 6:19].

Sorrowfulness (suffering) is a term that is more difficult to understand than appears at first sight. This is so for two reasons. First, sorrowfulness lies in the realm of experience, not that of rational knowledge. An object of rational knowledge, something physical, can be explained, but human experience cannot. It is easy to explain a tooth, but not a toothache. Toothache is an experience that is not communicable. One can imagine to some extent what a toothache means to another, if one has experienced it and to the degree that one has experienced it, but one will never know exactly the other's experience. With *dukkha*, human suffering, we are in the realm of a similarly incommunicable experience. No picture of it can be drawn. Only allusion to it can be made. We can understand it only by our own experience of it.

The second difficulty is that our ordinary perception of suffering focuses only on its corporeal aspects. Books and newspapers speak of suffering in hospitals, on battlefields, from unemployment, starvation, or floods, but suffering has another dimension-a mental dimension. The same illness affects different persons differently, depending on the mental attitude of each. An individual's mental attitude increases or reduces the degree of pain endured. This is an important factor to be remembered in grasping the reality behind the First Noble Truth. Gautama's analysis is at a psychological level.

If the psychological dimension is ignored, a statement such as "Birth is sorrowful, growing old is sorrowful, disease, death are sorrowful" may be misunderstood, for Gautama did not bring liberation from birth, old age, disease, or death in the *physical* sense. He himself succumbed to these, as does every other human being.

Within his statement lies an insight to a human reality that is unquestionably true. In the matter of growing old, one's attitude toward one's age may illustrate what is meant thereby. When someone's name is asked, it is given very readily, but if the same person's *age* is asked, the response is not so spontaneous. If the questioned person is a man approaching his forties or, in our "youth-oriented" society, a woman approaching her thirties, the natural tendency is to change the topic of conversation, or to hint at an age several or many years below the real one! The same reaction may follow for one who discovers the first gray hairs that are beginning to appear or who hears from a companion the remark, "that's a sign of old age!" His inner reaction will be neither joy nor indifference. The ordinary person shudders at the very thought of growing old.

The second part of Gautama's statement reveals even more deeply the psychological dimension of human misery. "Union with the unpleasing, separation from the pleasing, is sorrowful; the wish which cannot be fulfilled is sorrowful."

A fundamental fact of experience is that more persons suffer from problems of love and hatred than from sickness, famine, and wars. No elaborate case study is required for proof. Familiarity with everyday life will provide sufficient proof. Here is a man who has loved one woman and circumstances have led him to marry another. Another woman loves a man and lives the whole time in fear and doubt as to whether the man will love her in return. A third has loved a woman vehemently in the past and now lives in fear of her. In one household, children dread the moment that their father returns from work, and in another the husband prefers to remain in his office rather than in the company of his wife. "Union with the unpleasing, separation from the pleasing" have, from time immemorial, evoked the greatest flood of human tears. "The wish that cannot be fulfilled" too has caused humanity to endure untold agony.

The Pali expression rendered here as "desirous transient individuality" is *panca upadanakkhanda*. Literally it means the "five object-gripping aggregates" that constitute human nature. The expression is used to give the suggestion that love and hatred are ingrained in human nature, making suffering inevitable. Anyone aware of the tensions, fears, frustrations, and loneliness that persons endure throughout their lives will grant that suffering is an ingrained element of human nature.

To capture correctly Gautama's analysis of the plight of human existence, one must be able to distinguish between the external physical personality of an individual and the inner invisible personality. The latter can be very sick or deformed whereas the former is in perfect health and quite pleasant-looking. In caricature form, the inner mental personality of individuals in contrast to their physical personality would appear somewhat as in **Figure 1** (see next page).

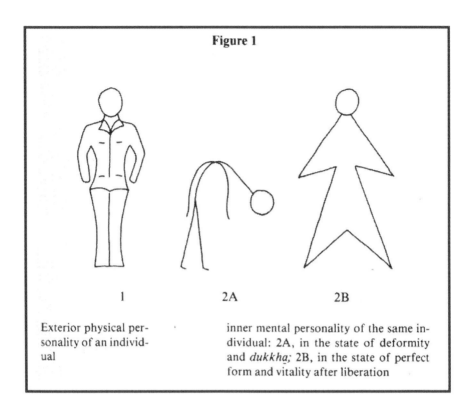

Figure 1

1	2A	2B

Exterior physical per-
sonality of an individ-
ual

inner mental personality of the same individual: 2A, in the state of deformity
and *dukkha;* 2B, in the state of perfect
form and vitality after liberation

Modern society, in particular, provides ample proof of the veracity
of the First Noble Truth. Speaking of modern American society
and its search for identity, John Powell says:

Human nature abhors a vacuum. And in this moment the ache of
emptiness inside man is obvious in the shocking statistics on our
national mental health. Two-thirds of all the hospital beds being
occupied at the moment in America are occupied by mental
patients. More than one out of every ten Americans has already
undergone some form of psychotherapy. More than one out of
every ten college students is estimated to be so emotionally
crippled, that it will be impossible for him to finish his education
[Powell, 36].

If in a country as economically developed as America the inner
malady of humanity has not been cured, we can imagine how deep

25

the ailment is. What is strange is that the same unrest is found in economically poor Asian and African countries too. If human unrest afflicts rich or poor alike, its roots must be deeper than the individual's economic situation. It is a situation universally true of all humankind and internal to each human being.

Christianity, too, recognizes the abnormality of the fallen nature of humankind and traces the "fall" to a sin committed by the first couple, Adam and Eve. All humankind has inherited the consequences of this "original sin." Judaism speaks of the "evil impulse," the *yetzer ha ra*, in every man and woman.

In the field of science, too, this fact has not passed unnoticed. There are adherents of the theory of evolution who seem to think that this state is a consequence of the imperfect stage of human evolution. Reason, which is newly developed in it, is not yet fully developed; the senses and reason are not fully coordinated.

In summation, the doctrine of the First Noble Truth states: for one reason or another, whatever that reason may be, something is wrong with humanity. It is crippled. It is suffering. It is sorrow-full.

Chapter Four

Cause of Sorrow: Second Noble Truth

Just as the human malady was defined by Gautama in one word (*dukkha*, or sorrow), so was its diagnosis. The word is *tanha*, which could be translated greed, voluptuous desire, craving. The Second Noble Truth states the cause of suffering:

> Again, monks, this is the Noble Truth as to the origin of sorrow; it is the recurring greed, associated with enjoyment and desire and seeking pleasure everywhere which is the cause of this sorrow. In other words, it is the greed for sense pleasure, greed for individual existence, greed for non-existence [VP/MV, 10, i, 6:20].

According to this Noble Truth, greed, which is at the root of human suffering, has three forms. In English, they are traditionally rendered (a) greed for sense-pleasure, (b) greed for individual existence, (c) greed for nonexistence (in Pali: *kama tanha, bhava tanha, vibhava tanha*).

Greed for sense-pleasure. This first type of greed can be taken as a reference to the fierce yearning that all human beings experience in their effort to satisfy the desires of the senses. This yearning is most evident in the area of the two principal self-protective instincts in human beings: the instincts for food and for sexual satisfaction. Food consumption and sexual relationships are the most essential and the most justifiable activities of human life. They are fundamental to human survival as individuals and as a species. Nevertheless, there are no other areas in which human beings are so incapable of achieving a proper balance. In either sphere, greed outdoes need. Thus, the very instincts that should

27

protect women and men tend to hurt them. The tendency to overeat and to overindulge oneself in sexual pleasure seems more natural than the healthy use of these instincts.

Gluttony and unchastity are weaknesses that are almost natural to humans. A human being facing an appetizing plate of food, or an attractive member of the other sex, experiences reactions that are almost beyond control. It is to this inner, almost wild, force that Gautama refers by *kama tanha*, greed for sense-pleasure.

Greed for individual existence. The second type of greed mentioned by Gautama is greed for existence (*bhava tanha*). The existence implied by the Pali term *bhava* is very different in meaning from the same word as used in Western philosophy or even in ordinary conversation. In both Western philosophy and current usage "existence" designates the state of being in its most general and unqualified form. It can be predicated of something in complete disregard to whether its state of "being" is good or bad, pleasant or painful. Because of that very generic connotation, it can be used equally and indifferently of a stone, a tree, a human being, or God.

Bhava on the contrary has a very specific psychological connotation. It refers principally to the pathological state of human existence or, in other words, to human existence as characterized by the tendency to be possessive. That is why *bhava*, unlike the term "existence," cannot be used generally in reference to a stone or a tree. It can be used only of a being endowed with senses.

The ultimate aim of any being endowed with senses is greater and greater sense-gratification. This is a human target that can never be fully achieved. The closer one gets to it, the further it recedes. This is so evident in the daily search for comfort. Men and women seek to be increasingly comfortable day by day and are not satisfied today with what they found to be comfortable yesterday. Yesterday they were satisfied with a wooden chair, today they need a cushioned chair, and tomorrow they will need a rocking chair.

It is existence in this pleasure-searching form that is referred to by the term *bhava*. This is a clarification that Jewish and Christian students of Buddhism should keep well in mind from the outset. Otherwise the danger of their misunderstanding important Buddhist assertions is very great.

With the aim of preventing misunderstanding of the term *bhava*, many Buddhist manuals resort by preference to the rendering "becoming" rather than to "existence." But a closer rendering would be "greedful existence," or better still "emotional existence." Attachment to a form of "emotional existence" is not compatible with a life of inner peace and mental rest. It is this emotional form of existence that Gautama constantly emphasized should be terminated and done away with if liberation from *dukkha* is to be experienced in its perfect form.

Greed for non-existence. "*Vibhava tanha*," which Gautama sets down as a third form of greed to be avoided, is one whose sense is a little less self-evident. It is rendered in the commentary literature as "craving for annihilation or non-existence." Gautama was very likely referring to the meaningless craving of religious persons after rigid forms of asceticism. Asceticism, as was practiced by the very monks that he was addressing, was so injurious to life that it easily amounted to a form of self-destruction.

It is, however, also not impossible that the word *vibhava* in its pre-commentary usage would have had an altogether different meaning. It may have been used in the sense attributed to it in the dictionary. There the word means wealth, property, material prosperity. If so, *vibhava tanha* would refer to a deep-seated desire to hoard more and more material goods, more and more wealth. Humans desire to possess more and more, forgetting that the greatness of humanity lies not in what a person has, but in what a person is. Goods are, in popular human judgment, more pleasurable than is goodness.

Thus, there would be three types of greed that correspond to the three fundamental human appetites: concerning the senses, emotions, possessions. As we shall see later, these three appetites are to be brought under control by what for Gautama—and many other thinkers—is the supreme human faculty, the mind, reason.

Whatever be the original sense of the third type of greed, there is no doubt as to the nature of the overall psychological insight of Gautama. With his notion of *tanha*, greed in its multiple forms, he has pointed to the sickest aspect of the human tragedy. A human being is, as it were, constitutionally a victim of greed.

If presented in caricature, the root cause of the intrinsic human malady could be pictured as a human bound by a strong chain to objects of sense-pleasure, shown in Figure 2 (see next page) as a large diamond. Such an image would have been in the mind of the Buddha when he stated:

> Monks, I do not see any other single chain by which beings for a long time wander and hurry through the round of emotional existence, like this chain of greed (*tanha samyojanam*). Truly, monks, beings wander and hurry through the round of emotional existence bound by this chain of greed [*Itivuttaka*, Vagga II, Sutta 5].

Figure 2

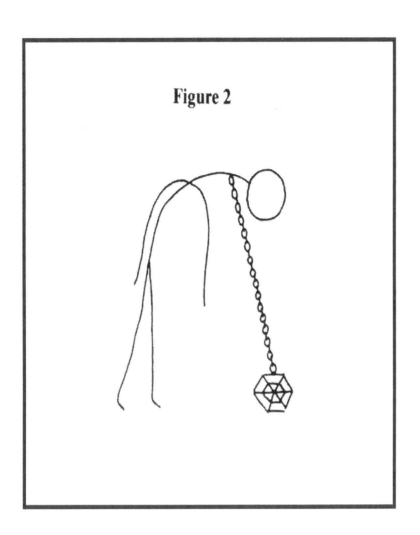

Chapter Five

Emotionalism in Knowledge

To see more fully the justifiability of Gautama's thesis on the greed-fulness of the human being, it would be of great help here to consider how human cognition was explained in the Indian philosophy of Gautama's day. It is an analysis that Gautama himself referred to on numerous occasions.

According to this explanation, commonly referred to as the Name-Form (*nama rupa*) theory, a human being is a composite of two realities. On the one side is the bodily form (*rupa*) consisting of the senses. On the other is "name" or individuality proper. Persons receive their individuality from the way their senses act. "Name" is thus a reference to the act of human cognition, or the action of the senses. The activation process of the senses is in its turn further divided into four categories or stages. Graphically put, the division and subdivision are as in **Figure 3**.

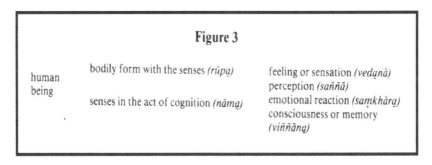

Figure 3

human being	bodily form with the senses *(rūpa)*	feeling or sensation *(vedanā)*
		perception *(saññā)*
	senses in the act of cognition *(nāma)*	emotional reaction *(samkhāra)*
		consciousness or memory *(viññāṇa)*

Taken altogether, an individual is said to consist of "five aggregates": bodily form, feeling, perception, emotional reactions, and consciousness.

Bodily form (rupa). The physical form, composed as it is of the four elements that constitute all material objects—namely, earth, water, fire, and air (*patavi, apo, tejo, vayo*)—is the container of sense organs. According to the Indian calculation there are six sense-organs in all: the eye for seeing, ear for hearing, tongue for tasting, body for touching, nose for smelling, and mind for imagining. In the process of cognition, each of the senses passes through the four stages of feeling, perception, emotional reactions, and consciousness.

Feeling (*vedana*). When any sense organ comes in contact with an external object, it senses or feels the presence of the object. This is the first step in its process of cognition.

Perception (*sañña*). In the second step, the sense organ recognizes the object for what it is. It perceives a rose as a rose and a scorpion as a scorpion. But what is very vital to remember here is that, according to the Indian view, perception does not stop with an objective concept of the object. The senses do not record any object with the impartiality of a camera. They also recognize it as something either desirable or obnoxious. The sense organ, in the act of perception, as it were, says: this is a rose, how beautiful! This is a scorpion, how dreadful!

Emotional reactions (Sanskrit: *samskhara*; Pali: *samkhara*). This refers to the reactions that take place within the cognitive faculty as a result of the perception of a sense-object. English translators have rendered the term *samskhara* as "mental formations" or "volitional formations." But the reality implied by it would be better captured by a simpler expression such as "emotional reactions."

The term "emotion" comes from the Latin verb *emovere* (*e-movere*), which means to move out. And emotion is in reality the action, or better, reaction, of being moved through the feelings of either love or hate, out of oneself toward the perceived object. The emotional reaction of either love or hate is, according to Indian philosophy, an innate element of sense-knowledge. According to the Indian view, the senses can never stop with the perception of a rose as a rose or of a scorpion as a scorpion. It has inevitably to

33

react to it. It has, as it were, to say: "Oh! a beautiful rose, I love it," or "Oh! a dreadful scorpion, I hate it."

This love-hate dimension of sense-knowledge (in its third stage) should show us clearly why Gautama attached so much importance to the notion of *samskhara* and constantly warned his hearers about its dangers. According to him, *samskhara* is at the root of *karma* itself, and almost identical with it. *Karma* (close in concept to the popular idea of sin) refers to that disoriented form of human behavior that brings with it very low forms of mental existence. Whatever be the expression adopted in rendering the term *samskhara* into English, the emotion-packed nature of sense knowledge in this stage should not be lost sight of if the reality beneath it is to be fully grasped.

Consciousness or memory (*viññana*). *Viññana* in its generic sense means deep knowledge (vi-ñana); but it is deep knowledge of the rational type, the source material of which comes from the senses. It is different from deep knowledge of the religious type called *vidassana* or "insight," based on the act of reflection on one's own self and life. *Viññana* has in it all the emotional elements common to knowledge gained from the senses, and so in this context it could be referred to as a storehouse of emotional reactions. For easier understanding, it could be referred to as memory too. *Viññana* as a memory keeps enclosed within it all the love-hate experiences that an individual has undergone. According to the Theravada Buddhist explanation, it is such a memory that passes from one life to another in rebirth. The love-hate emotional reactions stored in it determine the high or low nature of the individual's new birth.

This analysis of the human individual should make it very clear that the Indian, and particularly the Buddhist, approach to human existence is a very pragmatic one. It defines existence through the personal experience of existence. In that sense, the Buddhist approach has something in common with that of Descartes, the Western philosopher who lived only three centuries ago. Descartes defined existence with reference to a human being's experience of the act of thinking: "I think, therefore I exist" (*Cogito ergo sum*). By this reference to thinking, Descartes described human existence at its highest level of experience.

But Gautama looked at existence from a more concrete level of human experience. If paralleled with the Descartes formula, Gautama's is somewhat as follows: "I am greedy, I love, I hate, therefore I exist." For Gautama, greed and emotional reactions—or better, the greed that produces emotional reactions—is something inherent to a human being's perception of external objects. If greed is inevitable because it is a constitutional element of human cognition, then *dukkha* or mental uneasiness is itself inevitable.

Chapter Six

Doctrine of Dependent Origination: A Cause of the Greed That Causes Sorrow

Gautama was not satisfied with simply asserting that greed is the cause of human sorrow or that greed is something ingrained in human nature. He wanted to go further and also show how greed caused suffering. This he did through an exposition very fundamental to Buddhist thought known as the doctrine of Dependent Origination (Pali: *paticca samuppada*; Sanskrit: *pratitya samutpada*). In it he points out that greed effects sorrow through a chain of intermediary causes and that greed itself, in its turn, is only an effect. Because sorrow originates from and is dependent upon a number of interconnected causes, this doctrine is termed "Dependent Origination" or "Chain of Causality."

Gautama considered this formula very fundamental to his teaching. He considered it so fundamental that he once said of it: "If anyone understands the doctrine of Dependent Origination, he knows what my teaching is" (MN, I, 190, Sutta 28).

Gautama first expounded it in answer to a question posed by the ascetic Kassapa. Having heard of Gautama's analysis of the cause of human suffering, he asked: "Venerable Gotama, is sorrow self-wrought... or is it wrought by another... or otherwise is it arisen without a cause [i.e., fortuitously]?" (SN, II, 19; see also VP/MV, i, 1:1-2).

To each of these Gautama's answer was no. This apparently self-contradictory reply confused Kassapa. To illuminate Kassapa's confused mind Gautama expounded his theory according to which, even though sorrow is not caused by humans themselves or by anyone outside humans, it is not a matter of accidental occurrence. Humans suffer as the result of a mental process operating within their very being. At the root of this mental process is their ignorance (Pali: *avijja*, Sanskrit: *avidya*), which is why ignorance is set down as the first link of the chain of causes. The text of the formula reads:

1. Because of ignorance (*avijja*), emotional reactions (*samkhara*) arise.
   Because of emotional reactions, hate-love packed memory (*viññana*) arises.
   Because of [the transmission of] memory, again the emotional Name-Form structure (*nama rupa*) arises.
   Because of the emotional Name-Form structure, the six senses (*salayatana*) arise [i.e., their activity].
   Because of the [activity of the] six senses, contact (*phassa*) arises.
   Because of contact, feeling (*vedana*) arises.
   Because of feeling, craving (*tanha*) arises.
   Because of craving, clinging (*upadana*) arises.
   Because of clinging, once again the emotional existence [*bhava* or existence in low forms] arises.
   Because of emotional existence, aging arises, and death, sorrow, lamentation, pain, grief, and despair. Thus, does this entire mass of suffering arise. This is called the Noble Truth of the arising of suffering [SN, II, 19].

It must of course be admitted that this formula, however important it may be, is not, at least in the form it is found preserved in our present scriptures, very clear. Though the statements are supposed to be linked with each other, the links are not self-evident. It is not impossible that this might be due to a certain corruption that the text has undergone in the process of transmission at the hands of early transmitters and subsequent copyists. It is not likely that

37

Gautama, who was always concerned about presenting his teaching in a way easily understandable by ordinary persons, would have given it exactly in its present somewhat puzzling form.

Probably because of the repetition of a number of statements in the formula and as a way of explaining it, many early commentators considered this chain to be an elaboration not just of one life span but of three. The first and second statements refer to a past life, the third through the ninth to the present life, and the tenth to a future life or rebirth. It is, however, more likely that Gautama is referring not to different physical existences, but to different emotional existences of the same life span.

Even if the formula suffers from a certain lack of clarity, there is absolutely no doubt as to the central lesson it teaches. That lesson consists in two very vital elements. First, it affirms that craving, greed, is the cause of suffering. Secondly, it affirms that ignorance (ignorance of the "self") is the cause of greed.

Greed: the cause of sorrow. According to the first element, the uncontestable reason for the unhappiness of human beings is their voluptuous desire. Nonetheless—and this is the fact that it insinuates still more strongly—individuals themselves cannot be held responsible for it. Desire is not something that they freely develop within themselves. It is something they cannot escape from, for it is the natural outcome of a mechanical deficiency that is intrinsic to everybody's sense-cognition.

The senses of the ordinary unevolved human being are not under the control of reason. And as long as they are not under the control of reason, the senses tend to run amok in pursuit of sense-objects. This they do in a progressive degree of intensity. The gradation is indicated in the formula first as feeling, then as craving, and finally as clinging. This idea is expressed in the second half of the formula:

Because of the senses, contact (with the sensed objects) arises.

Because of contact, feeling (toward contacted objects) arises.

Because of feeling, craving (after the felt objects) arises.

Because of craving, clinging (to craved objects) arises.

Because of clinging, low forms of human behavior arise [SN, II, 19].

The inner connection between individuals' sense-knowledge and their emotional behavior should now be clear from the Name-Form analysis of human nature seen earlier. Nevertheless, there are a few links in the chain that call for a word of explanation.

The tenth or last link of the chain, for instance, says that "because of desirous existence, aging arises, as also death, sorrow, lamentation, pain, grief, despair." As is only too obvious, detachment from craving, even in its most perfect form, cannot save one from the common human fate of old age and death. Gautama and the *arahats*, the "perfect," themselves succumbed to old age and death. So, what Gautama implies here is not old age and death in their physical form, but the mental anguish that anyone unliberated from emotionalism experiences in the face of these humanly unavoidable realities. It is the mental anguish that is underlined by the terms "sorrow, lamentation, pain, grief, despair" given in the same statement.

It is this relationship between emotionalism and mental anguish that is underlined also by the second and third statements: "emotional reactions cause memory" and "memory causes name-form." The term "name-form" here does not necessarily refer to a new physical existence, but rather to a new emotional existence.

Thus, in the major part of this chain, what Gautama does is to repeat, using different terms each time, the fact of the connection between emotionalism and mental anguish. Terms such as *samkhara, nama rupa*, and *bhava* are really synonyms for the same reality of emotional existence.

Ignorance of "self": the cause of greed. But that is not the only conclusion that Gautama wants to bring out through this formula. There is something very new contained in this formula, not contained, for instance, in the Name-Form analysis. As a second important conclusion, the formula of Dependent Origination pinpoints *why* humanity so adamantly continues to behave emotionally. The reason as given in the very first statement is ignorance. Humanity is ignorant of the transience of material things on the one hand and of its mental processes on the other. Put more precisely, humanity has no right understanding of its "self." It is blind to the fact that it is a "no-self."

The doctrine of "no-self" is probably the most perspicacious teaching of Gautama and likely the one that is most exclusive to Buddhism. What Gautama understood by "no-self" needs to be studied separately. It will be taken up in chapter 9.

For our present purposes, it suffices to stress that Gautama in this formula has assigned a cause to human suffering beyond greed. Thus, in a nutshell Gautama's conviction expressed in the formula of Dependent Origination is: *because humanity is blind to the true nature of its "self," it behaves emotionally and is greedy for sense-gratification; and the continuance of this greed for sense-gratification makes it fall again and again into agonizing emotional states of existence.*

Christian and Jewish students should take care not to confuse the Buddhist doctrine of Dependent Origination with the Judeo-Christian doctrine of creation. Both are at times referred to, and quite un-introspectively, as the doctrine of "cause and effect." But in content and purpose the two are very different. The Buddhist doctrine of cause and effect pertains to the domain of psychology. It explains the process of the human act of cognition. The Judeo-Christian doctrine of creation lies in the domain of cosmology and ontology. The difference between them becomes clearer when we examine the aims of the two doctrines. The Buddhist doctrine seeks the cause of human mental anguish, whereas the Judeo-Christian doctrine seeks the cause behind the existence of the world and the human race—two very different purposes. This Buddhist doctrine would be closer to the Christian doctrine of original sin and the Jewish notion of *yetzer ha ra* than to that of creation.

The formula of Dependent Origination is in reality intended by Gautama to be a close follow-up to his sermon on the Four Noble Truths. Through it he says that even though humanity suffers due to an emotional form of existence, the situation is *not* irremediable: ignorance *can* be overcome. By the same token, he implies that liberation from suffering requires not penances or rituals, but simply the elimination of ignorance through an adult, enlightened form of life. According to Gautama, an enlightened view of life is all that is necessary to cure human beings of their innermost sickness. An enlightened view of life is of itself a medicine. For the deepest human sickness, no other medicine is necessary.

Chapter Seven

Retribution and Rebirth: Karma and Samsara

Besides the doctrines of Dependent Origination and Name-Form outlined in earlier chapters, there are two others that can throw much light on the teaching contained in the Second Noble Truth. They are the doctrines of *karma* (retribution) and *samsara* (rebirth). Together they show the moral and mental consequences of a life of greed.

When popular contemporary Buddhism is taken into account, these two doctrines are even more important than the earlier two. They play a more prominent part in the beliefs and practices of the majority of contemporary Buddhists. This is probably because *karma* and *samsara* predate Buddhism. They were found in Indian society long before Buddhism was born. As a matter of fact, these terms are so Indian in concept that it is almost impossible to find one-word equivalents for them in English. They are therefore safer retained in their original Pali-Sanskrit forms.

It is also important to remember that each of these terms is used by Buddhists and in Buddhist books in more than one sense. Both of them have, for instance, a popular sense and a more authentic sense. It is bes,t therefore, for students to be acquainted with all the different senses. Then, according to the context, they can judge which sense is intended.

Karma

Karma has at least three different senses.

1. Literally and etymologically it means action. In the broadest sense of the word, any action—eating, drinking, walking, sleeping—could be termed *karma*. However, it is its religious usage that we are concerned with.

In its religious usage, it refers to an action that has a moral or ethical value. *Karma* thus is good or bad actions presumed to result in an eventual reward or punishment either in this life or in a subsequent life.

In all Indian religions, as much as in Buddhism, good or meritorious actions are called *kusala karma*, and bad or demeritorious actions, *akusala karma*. In popular Buddhism, for purposes of religious instruction, ten actions are commonly considered demeritorious: (1) killing, (2) stealing, (3) sexual misbehavior, (4) lying, (5) slander, (6) harsh language, (7) gossip, (8) sloth, (9) hatred, (10) illusion.

2. According to a second meaning, *karma* is not an action but a law. It is the law of retribution that pursues human actions so as to bring reward or punishment for them. Because of the *karma* law, persons now pay for what they have done in a previous life, and they will pay in a subsequent life for what they are doing now. *Karma* as understood in all the Indian religions is a cosmic law as universal and as unchangeable as, for instance, the law of gravity. Under the force of that law, good never fails to be rewarded and evil never escapes being punished.

3. It is, however, the third meaning of *karma* that is of direct relevance to the doctrine of the Second Noble Truth. As in its second sense, here too it is a law of retribution, but it is a law of retribution whose application is restricted to just one sector of human society. It does not reach out to the good and bad actions of

all human beings, but exclusively to the actions of persons who are not yet liberated.

According to Buddhist philosophy, human beings by their behavioral patterns fall into one of two levels of human existence. One is that of *samsara*. Persons in that category are not yet liberated from craving or from emotionalism in their judgments. This does not mean that they are incapable of good actions. Nevertheless, their best actions—even such actions as almsgiving—are tainted with feelings of self-love. It is the actions of such persons that are governed by the law of *karma*.

Karma can reward the good actions of such persons by giving them after their death a rebirth even in a world of the gods. Gods themselves, however good they may be, are, according to popular judgment, beings who are not fully liberated from greed.

The other level is that of *nirvana* or enlightenment. Persons in that category—Gautama and the *arahats*—have either totally eradicated unhealthy emotionalism or at least are definitely on the path to it. The *karma* law has no power over them, for they do not act in the hope of reward or punishment, or of merit and demerit. The only reward they are concerned with, if it could be considered a reward, is the peace of mind that results from the performance of duty. The law that governs and protects the life of such persons is the law of *dharma* or righteousness.

It is *karma* in this third sense that is of particular relevance to us here for the understanding of the Second Noble Truth: Greed is the cause of suffering.

Samsara

Samsara etymologically means fluctuation or an aimless wandering about. Beings in *samsara* are in an aimless movement like a cork on the waves of the sea. They do not move themselves. They are being moved by the objects of their senses. Their lives are a continuous rotation around sense-objects. As Gautama says: "Truly, monks, beings do wander and hurry through the round of existence bound by the chain of greed" (*Itivuttaka*, 8, Vagga II, Sutta 5).

An individual's behavior in *samsara* as visualized by Gautama can be illustrated as in **Figure 4.**

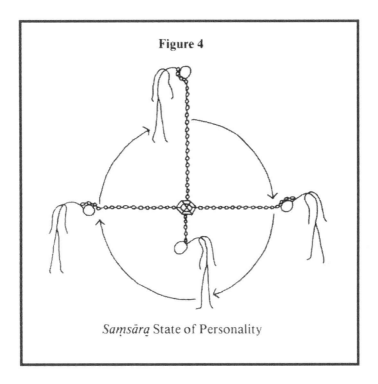

Figure 4

Saṃsāra State of Personality

The functioning of *samsara*, this continuous rotation around sense objects, has traditionally been explained by a process termed "rebirth." For a lucid understanding of the Four Noble Truths, and particularly of the very special type of liberation expounded therein, a clear grasp of the Buddhist version of rebirth is an indispensable prerequisite.

Our task of grasping the role of rebirth in Buddhism will be greatly reduced if we remember from the start that the Indian notion of rebirth, which was absorbed into Buddhism, could be interpreted in two very different and distinct ways. First, it could be interpreted in a physical sense. In that sense it referred to existence, or better, existences, outside the present life of an individual. These existences pertained equally to the period following death and that preceding birth. This is the sense in which a large number of Asians took it, and take it even today.

Secondly, rebirth could be interpreted in a moral sense. It then referred to the unwholesome— sometimes bad, but never perfect— thoughts that appear, disappear, and reappear in the mind of a person. Such mental transformations naturally occur within one and the same life span of an individual.

The basis for this second interpretation is nothing other than the very foundation of Indian philosophy itself. Indian philosophy is not concerned with the mechanics or the scientific analysis of birth, death, or existence. In this regard, Indian philosophy is different from Western philosophy. The latter is linked with science, the former with religion. The main concern of Indian philosophy is liberation through purification of the mind. Both liberation and the lack of liberation are basically states of mind. As Gautama himself said:

> I say to you the intention is itself *karma* [AN, III, 415].

> All things are mind-marshalled. Mind is their chief. And they are mind-made. If with an impure mind one speaks or acts, then suffering follows him even as a cart's wheel follows the hoof of the ox.... If with a pure mind one speaks and acts, happiness follows him like the shadow that never leaves him [*Dhammapada*, chap. I, 1-2].

46

Within the framework of Gautama's teaching on the Four Noble Truths, this second, moral, sense is the sense that has to be considered more authentic. The former is in no way compatible with his doctrine of liberation.

That of course does not imply at all that the first meaning is altogether alien to Buddhism. Anyone who has some acquaintance with the popular version of contemporary Buddhism will know how earnestly Buddhists believe in physical rebirth. Preexistence and reexistence are so much taken for granted by them that, in countries such as Tibet, Sri Lanka, and Burma, even daily newspapers continually report on past-life "memories" of little children.[3] Rebirth and its sister doctrine *karma* are so important to the Buddhist masses that popular Buddhism has at times been called a "*karma*-rebirth Buddhism."

One could of course suggest here that this fact be left out of consideration on the ground that popular Buddhism is not authentic Buddhism. After all, every religion has a popular as well as an authentic form, and in every religion the popular form has features that are foreign to the central tenets of that religion. Such a response could have provided a welcome relief had popular Buddhism been all that we had to reckon with.

Such a solution is, however, inadequate for the simple reason that even in the Buddhist scriptures we find references to rebirth in its physical form. On numerous occasions Gautama himself used the traditional concept of rebirth to make his lessons intelligible to the people. The book of Jataka stories is a very good example of this. This book is a collection of nearly five hundred fifty moral-value stories said to have been narrated by Gautama. At the end of each story Gautama is seen identifying himself with the hero of the story. A number of the heros in them are animals. This identification has led to the popular assumption that Gautama had five hundred fifty previous lives.

One way to confront this problem is to call in question the integrity of the scriptures by saying that there are contradictions in them, or that the rebirth texts found in them really are additions belonging to a subsequent era. But very likely the real reason for the complication in the Buddhist attitude to rebirth lies elsewhere. The root of it is largely in the complexity of the Indian notion of rebirth. Therefore, before undertaking to scrutinize the Buddhist attitude, we need to have a right grasp of the meaning and significance of rebirth in the Indian religious tradition.

A common belief in all Indian religions in their popular form is that a human being is born again and again in a number of lives; and it is not only as a human being that one is reborn. The *Chandogya Upanishad* has its version of the *karma-samsara* doctrine:

> Those whose conduct here has been good will quickly attain a good birth, the birth of a *brahmin* [member of the priestly caste], the birth of a *kshatriya* [member of the soldiery caste], or the birth of a *vaishya* [member of the merchant caste]. But those whose conduct has been evil, will quickly attain an evil birth, the birth of a dog, the birth of a hog, or the birth of a *chandala* [impure laborer] outcaste [*Chandogya Upanishad*, V, 10.7 (Radhakrishnan, 675)].

According to popular Buddhism, an imperfect being can, after death, be reincarnated in one of several worlds. One explanation enumerates five such states of existence: (1) the lower world (*duggati, vinipata, niraya*), (2) the animal kingdom (*tiracchanayoni*), (3) the spirit sphere (*petavisaya*) or the sphere of ghost-beings and demons, (4) the realm of human beings (*manussa-loka*), (5) the realm of gods (*devaloka*). The *devaloka* itself has several levels.

This popular belief in the possibility of a human being's rebirth in the form of a god, a human, a demon, or an animal may seem imaginative but, as any phenomenologist of religion would grant, behind such imaginative expressions is a recognition of deep

48

human realities that cannot be adequately expressed except in imaginative language.

Many today make a great mistake when they assume "rebirth" to be a word that has, like ordinary words, a self-contained sense. This is not so. "Rebirth" is not a word, for instance, like "pen," "pencil" or "paper." Such words can be understood in themselves, without reference to anything else. Rebirth, on the contrary, is an answer, and like the answer-words "yes" or "no," for example, it cannot be understood except in connection with the question to which it is related. And what is worse, rebirth is not an answer to just one question. It is a common answer to a number of questions. It is like a master key that can be used to open a number of doors. Further, those questions to which rebirth supplied an answer were not ordinary questions, but fundamental human questions. Three questions in particular occupied the Indian mind, and to all of them rebirth was the answer.

First, rebirth, and particularly its counterpart, preexistence (past lives), was the Indian answer to the question that could summarily be worded: Why do human beings suffer, and why do some suffer more than others? The Indian answer to this eternally baffling question was preexistence. Human beings are now reaping the fruits of their past actions. Belief in rebirth was thus a testimony that the ordinary Indian, even the one considered the most uneducated, was grappling with the great human dilemma of the inequalities of life.

The second question to which rebirth provided an answer was: Why should one do good and avoid evil in this life? For any ordinary person, it is not easy to find a self-evident reason for the doing of good and the avoidance of evil in this life. For all practical purposes, what is more evident is the contrary. Evil action brings greater and speedier prosperity in this life. The Indian answer was that of reward and punishment in a subsequent life. In that context, belief in rebirth was a testimony that the ordinary Indian was seriously grappling with the problem of human morality.

The third question to which rebirth provided an answer was: Is not perfection in the fullest sense possible to the human being? Achievement of perfection is an innate human desire, but concrete results always belied the expectation. Even at the door of death, every being is a very imperfect being. The Indian answer to this dilemma was rebirth. Perfection is a process that requires more than one life span. In that context, belief in rebirth was a proof that the ordinary Indian was grappling with the human problem of self-perfection.

Such an overall view of the popular Indian notion of rebirth should help us to see in a better light the problems connected with the Buddhist attitude to rebirth. First of all, it should help us to assess, with a greater sense of fairness, popular Buddhism that adheres so strongly to the doctrines of *karma* and rebirth. This is not to say that popular Buddhism is authentic Buddhism. That would not be true. Nevertheless, we have to admit that the belief of simple Buddhists in rebirth and *karma* is a sign that the greatest human problems have not escaped them. For that very reason, their version of religion does not deserve to be disdained.

Secondly, it helps us to understand Gautama's own attitude toward rebirth as well as the reason for the divergence in the scriptural assertions about that attitude. Gautama's own attitude, to begin with, is clear-cut. The questions that he had himself grappled with were practically the same as those to which rebirth was the answer. The problem of human suffering, the problem of human morality, the problem of human perfection, were also the problems he gave consideration to. But he looked at them from quite another angle, and provided an answer that was altogether different. For him, the problem and the answer pertained to the existence that a human being was presently experiencing. Intentionally, he kept out of his purview anything that preceded birth or followed death. Consequently, his version of liberation had nothing to do with actual preexistence or actual postexistence.

Nevertheless, he had too deep an understanding of human nature to be blind to the life questions behind the ordinary Indian's affirmation of rebirth. Out of respect for those questions, and the simple persons who posed them, he did not want to destroy abruptly and indiscriminately their idea of rebirth.

Further, he was a great educator, and being an educator, he knew how to use existing values even when presenting entirely new ones. It is also important for us to remember that he did not expound liberation in its most enlightened form haphazardly, anywhere and everywhere, or to anybody and everybody. He did so only when he realized that his listeners were ready for it; and so, to ordinary persons who were unprepared to follow his path fully he explained only those values of human goodness that were intelligible and useful to them. When addressing them, he naturally used the idea of rebirth that they were accustomed to.

Once those facts are granted, we cannot but repeat what was said earlier—namely, that rebirth, in its physical sense, is in no way a constituent element of Gautama's doctrine of liberation. This is a fact amply borne out by assertions in the Buddhist scriptures. A few indications are the following.

1. According to a belief popularly accepted in the India of Gautama's day, an individual was born in a higher or lower caste, or in different professions, as a result of actions in a previous life. Gautama strongly objected to that interpretation because it lessened personal responsibility in the present life. Nor did he believe in the superiority or inferiority of caste:

> Neither by ascetical hair-style, nor by caste, nor by birth, does one become a brahmin [a priest by caste]. The one who is truthful and righteous, such a one is a brahmin [*Dhammapada*, chap. 26, 11].
> By one's own action is one a brahmin, by one's own action is one a non-brahmin.
> By one's own action is one a farmer, an artist, a trader, a servant.

By one's own action is one a robber, a soldier, a king's counsellor, a king [MN, X, Brahmana Vagga VIII, Vasettha Sutta].

2. Because Gautama preached a liberation achievable in the present existence, preoccupation with either past or future existences was, in his view, an obstacle to the true goal. For him, only unenlightened, uneducated persons worried about such matters. In the Sabbhasava Sutta of the *Majjhima Nikaya*, he says:

> The uninstructed ordinary person, unskilled in the *Dhamma* [doctrine], thinks: Was I in a past period? Was I not in a past period? What was I in a past period? ... Now, will I come to be in a future period? Will I not come to be in a future period? What will I come to be in a future period? [MN, I, Mulapariyaya Vagga II, Sabbhasava Sutta].

3. Because Gautama's primary concern was the present existence, he made it very clear to his followers that virtue should never be practiced for the sake of benefits in an afterlife. A virtuous life was valuable for the very reason that it was the happier form of life right now.

This teaching is vividly brought out in a temptation story given in the Buddhist scriptures. According to that story, *Mara*, the Buddhist equivalent of the Judeo-Christian Satan, disguised as a brahmin ascetic, approached a group of Buddhist monks with the idea of diverting them from their way of life. *Mara* addressed the monks:

> "You, monks, you are still boys, young and black-haired, in the flush of youth. You are in the prime of life and have not amused yourself with worldly pleasures. Enjoy, good sirs, here and now, human pleasures. Do not abandon the

tangible pleasures of this life in expectation of uncertain joys in an after-life."

To this, the monks answered:

"We have not abandoned the present life, brahmin, for the sake of an after-life. We have abandoned what is less joyful in this life for what is more joyful in this life. The Lord has said worldly joys are third-rate joys. They produce suffering, despair, and disappointment. The life of the *Dhamma*, on the contrary, gives a more sublime and more stable type of joy that we can experience here and now."

When they had so spoken, the evil one departed shaking his head.... Then those monks approached the Lord, and told him what had transpired. The Lord said: That was no brahmin, monks, that was *Mara*, the evil-tempter come to cloud your clarity of vision [SN, Sagatha Vagga IV, Mara Samyutta].

From teachings of Gautama such as these it should become evident that physical rebirth is not a doctrine advocated by Gautama. It was in no way an element in his path to liberation. As Venerable Punnaji Thera, a Theravada Buddhist scholar, rightly observes:

Genuine Buddhism therefore is not "Karma and Rebirth Buddhism." Genuine Buddhism, which is independent of time (*akalika*), speaks not about rebirth, but about suffering (*dukkha*), and its cessation here and now [Punnaji Thera, 35].

All this conflict and confusion with regard to the doctrine of *samsara* and rebirth disappear when it is taken in its more authentic sense. According to that sense, what *samsara* is concerned with is not physical rebirth of individuals, but their moral rebirth, or their rebirth in different levels of emotional behavior; and such rebirths take place not after a person's death, but within the present life.

Venerable Buddhadasa Thera of Thailand makes that fact very clear in his book *Two Kinds of Language*. To him, the real meaning of rebirth is not the higher or lower physical birth that follows death, but the higher or lower forms of mental birth in the same existence. To bring that out he distinguishes between the popular interpretation of the doctrine and its real meaning:

> Birth as a beast means in popular language actual physical birth as a pig, a dog, or some other actual animal. Rebirth after death as some kind of lower animal is the everyday meaning of rebirth into the realm of beasts. In *dhamma* language it has a different meaning. At any moment when one is stupid, just like a dumb animal, then at that moment, one is born to the realm of beasts. It happens right here and now. One may be born as a beast many times over in a single day. So, in *dhamma* language, birth as a pig means stupidity [Buddhadasa Thera, *Language*, 21].

Put more succinctly, *samsara* in the deeper and the more authentic sense of the word is the *cycle of births and rebirths of the animal in the human*. It is from such a *samsara* and from such a law of *karma* that Gautama wanted to liberate human beings.

Chapter Eight

Nirvana: Relief from Mental Anguish: Third Noble Truth

Buddhism has at times been referred to as a pessimistic religion. This is because Gautama spoke in no uncertain terms about the situation of humanity as one of persistent inner sorrow. Our study of the first two Noble Truths shows how forcefully Gautama has done so. But those who think that Buddhism is pessimistic fail to realize that Gautama spoke of human sorrow solely because he wanted to teach others an escape from it. It is this escape from sorrow that is spotlighted in the Third Noble Truth. When seen in the light of the Third Noble Truth, Gautama's teaching becomes not one of suffering, but one of liberation from suffering. The first two Noble Truths have no meaning except in terms of the Third Noble Truth. *Dukkha* (sorrow) and *tanha* (greed) must necessarily be taken with nirvana. When so taken, Buddhism becomes not a religion of pessimism but one of great optimism.

Nirvana

The Third Truth reads:

> This, monks, is the Noble Truth of the cessation of suffering: It is the complete cessation (*nirodho*), giving up (*cago*), abandoning (*patinissaggo*) of greed (*tanha*); it is release (*mutti*) and detachment (*annalayo*) from greed [VP/MV, 10, i, 6:21].

This statement leaves no doubt as to what constitutes liberation from sorrow and where it is to be found. Liberation from sorrow exists only where there is no greed. It is to emphasize that fact that

Gautama here uses five expressions identical in meaning: cessation of greed, giving up of greed, abandoning of greed, release from greed, and detachment from greed.

One could be a little surprised to notice that the word "nirvana" itself (in Sanskrit: *nirvana*, in Pali: *nibbana*), the traditional expression for liberation from sorrow, does not appear in the formulation of this Third Truth. The reason for that is a simple one. Though *nirvana* is the more popular term in use today, it is not the only term that Gautama used to designate the sublime state of happiness of the liberated individual. Nor is it even the word that he used most. In the book *Sutta Nipata*, for instance, the word *nibbana* is used only fourteen times, whereas the word *santi* (peace) is used twenty-nine times. Further, the word "nirvana" is not different in meaning from any of the five terms used in the Third Noble Truth. As Gautama says elsewhere, "Destruction of greed, greedlessness, eradication of greed, that is *nirvana*" (*Tanhakkhayo virago norodho nibbanam*) (AN, II, 34).

In itself, *nirvana* is not difficult to understand. But like *samsara*, *nirvana* too has both a vulgarized sense and an authentic sense. In the vulgarized sense—that is, in the sense in which it is more commonly taken by the Buddhist masses—*nirvana* is a place to go to after death. (The term "nirvana" in that aspect has undergone the same deformation in the course of the centuries as Jesus' Jewish term "reign of God" and the Rabbis' "reign of heaven." At variance with the original Jewish signification that Jesus and the Rabbis gave to these terms, for millions of Christian and Jewish believers the reign also became the kingdom, a place to go to after death.)

If Gautama's meaning is to be grasped, *nirvana* must not be cut off from his teaching on sorrow (*dukkha*) and the cause of sorrow (*tanha*), for according to him, release from sorrow is to be found exactly where sorrow is to be found. Both liberation and sorrow should be thought of in reference to one and the same human being existing concretely here and now:

In this very body that is six feet tall, with its consciousness and perception, I declare are the world [i.e., sorrow], its arising, its cessation and the path that leads to the cessation of the world [AN, II, 45].

If both sorrow and liberation from sorrow are to be understood as applying to individuals in their present existence, then to explain *nirvana* in terms of a life after death would be a gross misrepresentation of the thought of Gautama.

There is a very important clue showing clearly the meaning that Gautama attached to *nirvana*. It is the manner in which the common folk of Gautama's day employed the term. In that popular usage, it referred to a "cooling down" of anything that had in one way or another become hot. As Venerable Buddhadasa writes:

Applied to fire, it referred to the going out and becoming cool of the embers. In speaking of boiled or steamed rice which had been served from the cooking pot into an empty bowl and become cool, the word used is *parinibbana*. It was thus an ordinary word used in a general way for everyday worldly things to indicate something rendered harmless [Buddhadasa Thera, *Dhamma*, 34].

Once that common usage is kept in mind, it is not difficult to reconstruct what Gautama implied by the term. As Trevor Ling explains it:

Nirvana is cessation of all passion, and because evil passion is regarded in Buddhist thought as a kind of fever, its cessation may be thought of as a "cooling down" after fever, a recovery of health. In fact, in Buddha's time the associated adjective *nibbuta* seems to have been an everyday term to describe one who is well again after an illness. It is evident from this that the original

Buddhist goal *nirvana* was the restoration of healthy conditions of life *here and now* [Ling, 136].

Fire is an image that can be looked at in two ways. In one way fire is good: it gives light and warmth. In another way, it is harmful: it burns and destroys. In Buddhism, it is the second aspect that is taken into account. Humankind is like a forest in flames. In the *Vinaya Pitaka* Gautama depicts the life of the person of greed:

> All is burning, all is in flames; and what is the "all" that is in flames, that is burning? The eye is burning. Visible objects are burning. Eye consciousness is burning. Eye-contact is burning. Feeling whether pleasant or painful, or neither pleasant nor painful that arises with eye-contact as its condition, that too is burning.
>
> With what are they burning? With the fire of craving, with the fire of hate, with the fire of delusion. They are burning with birth, aging, and death, with sorrow, lamentation, pain, grief, and woe.
>
> Similarly, the ear is burning...
> the nose is burning...
> the tongue is burning...
> the body is burning...
> the mind is burning....
>
> Seeing thus, the wise become dispassionate towards the eye, visible objects, eye-consciousness, eye-contact, and feeling ... become dispassionate towards ear, nose, tongue, body, and mind; ... through dispassion greed fades away. With the fading away of greed, his mind is liberated. When his mind is liberated, there comes the knowledge that it is liberated [VP/MV, chap. 1, 12:1-4].

The fire here refers to the impulsiveness, emotionality, and frivolity that cohabit a life of greed. A greedy person's life and time are burned up by sense-desire. Coolness stands for the life of tranquility. *Nirvana* is that tranquility. As the *Dhammapada* says: "There is no fire like passion, no ill like hatred. There is no sorrow like emotional individuality. There is no happiness higher than tranquility" (*Dhammapada*, chap. 15, 6). This life of "burning" through passions is what Gautama referred to as *samsara*. The "cooled down" life was for him *nirvana*. Therefore, it is wrong to look at *samsara* and *nirvana* as places or spheres beyond death. They represent two states of personality or two behavioral patterns. They are two states of life that the same individual can experience here and now.

The personality transformation outlined by the doctrines of *samsara* and *nirvana* are illustrated in **Figure 5**.

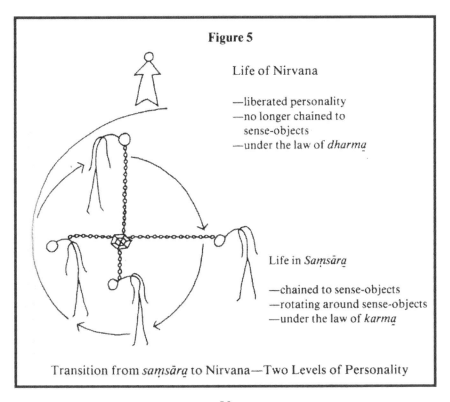

Figure 5

Life of Nirvana

—liberated personality
—no longer chained to
  sense-objects
—under the law of *dharma*

Life in *Saṃsāra*

—chained to sense-objects
—rotating around sense-objects
—under the law of *karma*

Transition from *saṃsāra* to Nirvana—Two Levels of Personality

With *samsara* and *nirvana*, we are in the domain of human transformation or, put differently, the humanization of the animal in human nature. The truth of this rather intriguing statement will become still clearer if we study the Buddhist explanation of the four stages of perfection, an explanation that corrects the impression that the transition from *samsara* to *nirvana* is instantaneous or an effortless step forward.

The transition from *samsara* to *nirvana* does not take place automatically or, as it were, overnight. The broad stream of mental purification has first to be crossed. The basic breakaway from *samsara*, of course, does come at one specific moment, upon the achievement of an intensive insight into the reality of life. At that moment, without any doubt, one realizes intuitively and not just rationally that the failure of one's past life is due to greed and self-centeredness, and that true joy and liberty will come when one is no longer "greed-full" or "self-full."

This convincing (and converting) awareness of reality (*vidya*, knowledge) is the doorway by which a person steps out of the territory of *samsara*, but *nirvana* in its fullness is not yet achieved. Full *nirvana* or "arahatship," perfect humanness, can be reached only by passing through three more preliminary stages. The four stages to perfection are characterized by: (1) *sotapanna* or *sovan*, literally, the stream-enterer; (2) *sakadagami*, the once-returner; (3) *anagami*, the non-returner; (4) *arahat*, the perfect one.

The *sotapanna* (stream-enterer) is one who has escaped from the samsaric level of personality and entered the stream that leads to perfection. As one escapes from the samsaric level (i.e., the state of greed), the heavy chain that once bound one to sense-objects is broken. The breaking of the main chain does not mean that one is now fully free. Habits of attachment and age-old illusions do not vanish quickly. Although the iron chain is broken, the mind remains attached to earthly objects by less firm cords or ropes.

Gautama enumerates ten such cords of bondage (*dasa satmyojana*) with which one who has escaped from *samsara* is still bound.

These cords have to be broken gradually, as one passes from one stage of perfection to another. The ten cords are: (1) self-illusion or pride, (2) doubt or flimsiness of mind, (3) trust in the superstitious power of rites and ritual, (4) desire for sense-gratification, (5) hatred or ill will, (6) desire for physical goods, (7) desire for nonphysical objects such as power and prestige, (8) self-conceit, (9) restlessness or aimless rushing about, (10) ignorance.

The *sotapannas* (stream-enterers), or those who are in the first stage, have broken the first three of these cords. Their moral behavior is perfect; they abstain from killing, stealing, adultery, lying, and the use of intoxicants. But their minds are not perfectly clear of doubt and their determination not fully strong; and so they can temporarily regress into *samsara*, the old life of greed. They could, as is said, regress as many as seven times, but they will never again be permanently fallen beings.

As they acquire greater insight into the realities of life, they enter the second stage, by weakening (though not totally rupturing) two other cords (4 and 5). This second stage, that of *sakadagamis* (once-returners), is more firm than the first and the possibility of their regression into a life of greed (*samsara*) is greatly reduced. They can, as the texts say, fall back, but only temporarily and only once. In the third stage, that of *anagamis* (nonreturners), they break fully the two cords that were only weakened in the earlier stage. Sense-desire and ill will are two ties that are not easily broken in a single effort. Once these are totally broken there is no danger whatsoever of regression into *samsara*. They still have five more small ties to break (6-10). By breaking these, they enter the stage of *arahatship* (see Piyadassi Thera, 210).

The process of self-perfection can be depicted as a crossing over from the shore of *samsara* to the shore of *nirvana*, in **Figure 6.**

Figure 6

Saṃsāra   Stream   Nirvana
(shore)   (of mind-   (shore)
                 purification)

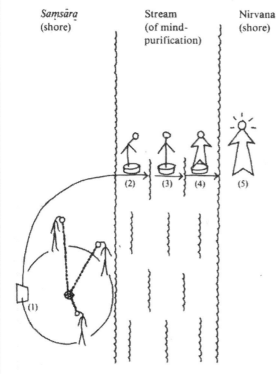

(1) Doorway to escape from
    saṃsāra: vidyā, knowl-
    edge.
(2) Sotāpanna (stream-
    enterer); 3 of 10 bonds
    broken. Can drift back
    temporarily to the old
    shore.
(3) Sakadāgāmi (once-
    returner). Can fall back
    temporarily just once.
    Has still 7 bonds to
    break, but 2 are
    weakened.
(4) Anāgāmi (nonreturner).
    Still 5 bonds to break.
    Will never drift back.
(5) Arahat (perfect one).
    Fully liberated from all
    forms of greed. Is on the
    shore of nirvana.

Transition from Saṃsāra to Nirvana—Path to Perfect Humanness

Life after Death

This explanation of the four stages to perfection should leave us without any doubt that what Gautama implied by *samsara* and *nirvana* is purely and simply the process of maturation of the human being.

Therefore, it would be wrong to pose the question of whether a person who has achieved *nirvana* will live after death or not. But because the question of afterlife is posed again and again, there are four points that are deserving of reflection.

1. The etymological formulation of the term "nirvana" is admittedly negative. *Nirvana* means a "cooling off" of a passionate life—namely, of behavior that is inspired by greed. It is a life "without greed." A negative formulation by itself need not mean that the reality implied is negative. As Venerable Piyadassi, a Buddhist monk, says:

> Though negative terms are often used to define *nibbana*, they do not imply that *nibbana* is mere negation or annihilation of a self. After all, negation does not mean an absolute void, a vacuum, but simply the absence of something. An *arahat* who has realized *nibbana* is free from craving. Craving exists in him no more and this is not mere nothingness or annihilation of self [Piyadassi Thera, 69].

2. In Buddhism, as said before, the word for existence is *bhava*, and it denotes exclusively a desire-full or emotional existence. *Nirvana* puts an end to emotional existence. But the "end of an emotional existence" does not at all mean nonexistence or annihilation. If existence apart from greed and pain is attainable, then one has to say that a person in *nirvana* definitely survives.

3. The silence of Gautama regarding an afterlife may have been meant to fulfill a purpose that is very ethical and typically Buddhist

in character. Buddhism considers self-assertion in any form to be detrimental to its cause of liberation. Truly liberated persons will be so non-self-assertive as to be totally disinterested in their very existence. They will be so indifferent and so detached as not to worry whether their present life is short or long, or whether they will live after death or not. Viewed in that light, Gautama's silence on an afterlife is a way of underlining the degree of detachment required for a life of true inner peace and mental serenity.

4. Finally, as almost anyone will grant, undue concern about an afterlife easily distracts a person from the primary goal of life, which is self-maturation. After all, if there is an afterlife, self-maturation is the only way to guarantee it. There is no other. A coconut, for example, if it is mature and ripe will, when planted, have a new life as a tree. An immature coconut, even if planted, has no chance for such survival. Therefore, a coconut, if endowed with intelligence, would, in the very interest of survival, abstain from worrying about it. Rather, it would concentrate exclusively on the work of self-maturation in its present existence.

If we are not to miss the central teaching of Gautama, we should never forget that the transition from *samsara* to *nirvana* is not, as the ordinary believer visualizes, a transition from life to afterlife through death, but a transition that takes place during life within the minds of individuals themselves. It is the transition from one level of awareness to another—namely, from a purely emotional awareness to a completely intellectual awareness. It is to *nirvana*, as the level of the highest intellectual awareness, that Gautama referred when he said:

> Monks, there is the unborn, unoriginated, unmade, and unconditioned. Were there not the unborn, unoriginated, unmade, and unconditioned, there would be no escape for the born, originated, made, and conditioned. Since there is the unborn, unoriginated, unmade, unconditioned, there is an escape for the born, originated, made, conditioned... this indeed is the end of suffering [*Udana*, VIII, 3].

In Gautama's language, as is evident in his formula of Dependent Origination, "the made," the originated," "the conditioned," refer to the state of samsaric personality—that is, made, originated, and conditioned by greed and ignorance. There is thus a state of personality outside the causality of this blind and vicious greed. The Christian refers to a parallel state as a "life in the Spirit," and the Jew as "walking before God."

Characteristics of Nirvanic Personality

In contrast with *samsara*, *nirvana* is a renovation of life, a revitalization that brings about a new dynamism. Nirvanic personalities are endowed with great courage, boldness, and inner strength. This vitality of nirvanic personalities comes from the very power of *dharma* (or *dhamma*), the power of truth and goodness to which they adhere.

Dhamma is a power that *protects* saintly individuals. It upholds them in a miraculous way, as it were, and draws from within them powers that are almost supernatural. One example of its protective power is given in the *Vattaka Jatakaya* of the book of *Birth Stories*. Gautama was going through a jungle one day accompanied by a group of his disciples. While in the middle of the jungle they noticed a fast advancing jungle-fire. The monks were excited and were suggesting solutions that would have been absolutely impractical. Gautama calmed them and asked them to trust in the good acts they had performed and in the power of truth and goodness that prevails in the universe. The fire continued to advance and surprisingly burned the whole area around, leaving untouched the trees of the area in which they were. When the amazed disciples asked how this could have happened, Gautama explained the doctrine of the protective power of truth (Sanskrit: *satya-kriya*; literally, truth-action).

This little incident may help us to see how this power of the universe, called *dharma* law, protects goodness and the good

65

person, and how, because of it, a nirvanic personality can be bold and courageous before the worst adversities of life.

The life of the nirvanic personality is also one of joy and inner peace. This is evident from the very words used by Gautama to describe *nirvana*: sorrow-lessness (*asokam*), security (*khemam*), purity (*suddhi*), sublimity (*panitam*), peace (*santi*), release (*vimutti*). All these characteristics are the natural outcome of a life of "greed-lessness, hate-lessness, folly-lessness" (*alobha, adosa, amoha*) (AN, I, 135, 195, 203; II, 192).

Four other virtues which are in themselves the result of a life of selflessness, but which are shown as the distinguishing marks of a Buddhist saint, are friendliness or loving kindness (*metta*), gentleness (*mudita*), compassion toward the suffering (*karuna*), and equanimity (*upekkha*) vis-à-vis fortune and misfortune. These are nirvanic virtues that Christian and Jewish students should keep in mind when they compare a Buddhist *arahat* to a Christian saint and a Jewish *zaddik*.

A very lucid exposition of the quality of life characteristic of the nirvanic personality is the following one given in chapter 15 of the *Dhammapada*. The words put into the mouths of Buddhist saints show clearly that *nirvana* stands for an authentic, integrated, and dynamic form of life:

> Happily, indeed, we live without hate among the hateful. We live free from hate amidst those who are hate-filled.

> Happily, indeed, we live in good health among the ailing. We live free from disease amidst those who are diseased.

> Happily, indeed, we live un-anxious among the anxious. We live free from anxiety amidst those who are anxious.

We who possess nothing live happily, indeed. We
will be feeding on happiness like the radiant gods.

Victory in material things breeds hatred. The
defeated lie in sorrow; whoever is peaceful lies in
happiness by giving up victory and defeat.

There is no fire like lust, no crime like hatred.
There is no sorrow like emotional existence, no
happiness higher than tranquility.

Hunger is the worst of diseases, emotional
existence the worst of sorrows; to whoever knows
this really, *nibbana* is the highest bliss.

Health is the highest gift, contentment the greatest
wealth, the trustworthy person the best of
kin; *nibbana* is the supreme bliss [*Dhammapada*,
chap. 15, 1-4].

Nirvana and Modern Life

Values such as these should remove any remaining doubt as to the
meaning of *nirvana*. *Nirvana* denotes a well-developed personality
or humanness in its ideal form. When so defined, *nirvana* is bound
to come alive with a renewed message even to our contemporaries
in modern society.

If this reality of *nirvana* is to gain credibility in the eyes of
contemporary individuals, two important responsibilities must be
assumed by modern teachers of religion. First of all, they should do
everything possible to uncover the concrete reality hidden within
old terminology and imagery. (This is applicable to the doctrines of
any religion.) After demythologizing and deconceptualizing these
doctrines, they can be reconceptualized in modern terminology
with contemporary images. Only then can the old doctrine be
appreciated by the modern person. In the matter of *nirvana* no

better terms can be proposed to make it relevant to modern times than those of ideal human maturity or mental health.

A second responsibility of religion teachers is equally important. They must remember that *nirvana* is primarily an experience and that the best way to teach it is to open the way for students to experience it even in a very limited degree. Theorizations on *nirvana* are of little help.

An example may help to illustrate, even though in an imperfect way, that *nirvana* can be experienced in one's day-to-day life. Rita was an 18-year-old Christian girl who faced a very severe personal problem. Her father owned a pharmacy and was financially well to do. He had a large car and a beautiful house, both of which she cherished very much. But soon after her father's death, her mother became interested in the manager of the pharmacy and married him. Rita resented this marriage very deeply. As she viewed it, the marriage made her lose everything she cherished—her mother, the house, the car. Unable to stand the sight of the step-father, she broke down completely and, with a sense of bitterness, left the house to reside with one of her uncles.

A few months later, she came across a book on Buddhism and was very much impressed by what she read. She learned for the first time that the cause of human suffering was greed and selfishness. A letter written after reading this book shows her reactions, which are quite insightful:

> I suffered so much because I was over-attached to mother, car, house, etc. And probably that is why I did not see anything except evil in mother's second marriage. Now after reading a book on Buddhism, and reflecting on Buddha's teaching, I see how wrong I was to have been so strongly attached to things that are so transitory. Now I care for my family. But I am no longer over-attached. As a result, I do not have the worries of the past. I am happy now. How true Buddha's teaching is!

The girl's reactions can give a glimpse into the type of mental state that Gautama envisaged in his teaching on *nirvana*. It shows at least that where there is less greed or attachment, there is less suffering. *Nirvana*, so understood, is simply a stage of adulthood and the transition from *samsara* to *nirvana* is really a transition from mental childishness to mental maturity. It is a stage when the senses and emotions are under the control of reason rather than the other way around, as is common among the majority of humankind. Much of the misery of life comes from the unrealistic, childish, undisciplined way in which men and women view life.

This childish view of life is called ignorance, *avidya*, by Gautama. *Nirvana*, in Gautama's own words, is nothing else but reality. "Reality, monks, is a name for *nirvana*" (SN, IV, 196).

In the section that follows, chapters 9-14, where the Fourth Noble Truth, the Eightfold Path, is studied, we shall see the form of conduct that leads to *nirvana* and eventually accompanies a nirvanic way of life.

Chapter Nine

Right Understanding: The Doctrine of the No-self

Of the Four Noble Truths, the most important by far is the fourth. In it Gautama announces the path leading to liberation—the Noble Eightfold Path—namely, Right Understanding, Right Thought, Right Speech, Right Action, Right Livelihood, Right Effort, Right Mindfulness, Right Concentration. In relation to this last truth, the first three are subsidiary. Their role is only to prove the validity and the acceptability of the Eightfold Path as a suitable path to liberation. Their purpose is to convince listeners that the eight steps of the path, however untraditional they may be in their simplicity, are by themselves—and without any accessories such as asceticism, rites or rituals, or worship of gods and goddesses—apt and adequate to ensure human liberation.

Presented in succinct form, the global message of the Eightfold Path is as follows:

1. Understand life correctly as transient, painful, and "selfless" (*samma ditthi*).

2. Think wholesome thoughts of detachment and good will (*samma samkappa*).

3. Use speech correctly without resorting to talebearing, harsh words, gossip, and lies (*samma vaca*).

4. Act correctly, abstaining from stealing, killing, and unchaste actions (*samma kammanta*).

5. Earn your livelihood without harming others (*samma ajiva*).

6. Strive constantly to keep your mind free from evil thoughts and filled with thoughts of detachment and friendliness (*samma vayama*).

7. Act mindfully, attentive to what you are doing each moment and conscious of the transience of life (*samma sati*).

8. Train your mind to restfulness and insight by periods of meditation (*samma samadhi*).

To understand more fully the Eightfold Path, each of these directives has to be examined in more detail. The ones that are more difficult for a Westerner to grasp—Right Understanding, Right Mindfulness, Right Concentration—will be treated a little at length in separate chapters. Others will be treated briefly.

Right Understanding

If Gautama had one ambition in life, it was to help persons lead lives more in keeping with the fullness of human nobility. Whatever he said or did had that as its sole target. His promotion of Right Understanding was directly aligned to it.

To help others perceive more clearly the right type of life they should lead, Gautama resorted to a very effective technique. He took the type of life that is conventionally upheld as ideal, and exposed its unwholesome characteristics in a pithy formula consisting of just three words: *anicca, dukkha, anatta*. Traditionally they are translated into English as "impermanent," "sorrowful," and "soul-less" ("self-less").

Even though the appropriateness of the English renderings, particularly of "soul-less" or "self-less" for *anatta*, needs to be reinvestigated, even in its traditional form it can give an inkling as to the purpose it was meant to serve. It was meant to arouse disgust with the atrophied type of lives most persons were leading. In spite of the brevity, the formula was a severe challenge to a value system that was assumed to be too ancient and too universal to be challenged,

The simplicity and brevity of the formula, however, should not blind us to the important place that it held in the philosophy of Gautama. The formula was central to his doctrine of liberation. There is hardly any major sermon of his that is not an elucidation of this formula, or does not at least contain a reference to it. Hence, it is essential that we discover its real meaning and significance.

If we are not to misunderstand this formula, we should from the very beginning keep in sight the exact nature of what Gautama is subjecting to analysis. We would be making a great mistake were we to think that the purpose of the formula is to analyze life in its physical form. Nothing is further from the truth. What is analyzed is not life as such, but a particular form of life pursued by many. It refers more to a fashion of life than to the fact of life. If we take the three words, one by one, we shall see this clearly.

The first term, *anicca*, is a word composed of the prefix *a*, an equivalent of the prefix "no" or "non" in English, and the adjective *nicca*, which means "lasting" or "permanent." And so *anicca* means "nonpermanent" or "nonlasting," "transient."

But the transience understood here is not the transience of life in a general sense—in the sense that all human beings come and go. They are born, they mature, grow old, and eventually die. But if that were the transience that is implied here, there would be nothing new about it. Even a child of ten would know that.

What Gautama is underlining is the fleeting nature of the pleasures that most persons try to fill their lives with. Satisfaction of one's own emotional desires is for the majority of humankind the supreme target in life. The sense of fulfillment that such persons' experience is of a very transient nature. It does not even cross their minds that life is capable of giving another form of human fulfillment, one that by comparison is much more lasting and much more satisfying.

Once we see the meaning of "transient" (*anicca*), it is not difficult for to grasp the meaning of the second word, "sorrowful" (*dukkha*). An emotion-dominated life, however contrary to popular judgment it may be, is in reality a sorrowful one. This does not mean that the satisfaction of emotional desires has no pleasure attached to it. Gautama did not deny the obvious. But he saw clearly that enjoyment of life had different depths and levels. There were for him superior joys and third-rate joys. The latter in comparison with the former were better described as "sorrow-full." Enjoyment of that type almost always brought in its wake only a sense of frustration and self-dejection.

The last term, *anatta*, expressed still another aspect of a third-rate form of life. Unfortunately, however, it is a term for which a one-word equivalent cannot be given, because the term has different usages. As a result, different interpretations have been given to it across the centuries by different Buddhist sects and schools of thought. To go beyond those interpretations and discover the original sense in which Gautama used it, effort and patience are necessary. But, because a correct grasp of Buddhism depends in large measure on a thorough understanding of it, the effort and the patience will be rewarded.

Anatta: Ambiguity of the Term

If we begin with the external form of the word, it is a composite term, like *anicca*. It is composed of the negating prefix *a* and the term *atta*. The letter *n* placed between them has no specific sense; its function is to make the pronunciation easier. Thus, taken as one word, *anatta* is the negative form of *atta*. It stands for a negation of whatever *atta* stands for.

Complication comes from the meaning of the word *atta*. It has two meanings, two completely different usages. Of these, one can be considered more important, in that it is the one that is more commonly used. In that usage, it is a word that has a place in the

73

ordinary person's day-to-day language, and does not carry with it any philosophical or speculative connotations.

In that meaning, the word (pronounced, as a rule, with the final *a* long-*atta*) is a reflexive pronoun with a distributive connotation. Equivalents in English are "one," "oneself," "each one." In English, such words are used to replace personal pronouns such as "we," "you," "they," "ourselves," "yourselves," "themselves." The term *atta* is often used adjectivally too. When so used it has a possessive sense, such as "of one's own." *Anatta*, used adjectivally, would mean "not of one's own." The term *atta* is a word of such everyday use that in the sentence "Each one must look after one's own umbrella," put into Pali, *atta* would be used for both "each one" and "one's own."

In the Pali Buddhist scriptures *atta* is very widely used in this sense. An obvious example is the "Treatise on Oneself" (*Attavagga*), which is the twelfth chapter of the *Dhammapada*. This chapter consists of just twelve verses of two lines each. Within that short space, the word *atta* appears sixteen times, and each time it is used in the above sense. One citation alone is sufficient to show its usage there: *atta hi attano nato* ("each one [must be] a protection to himself/herself").

The second usage of the word *atta* (with the final *a* pronounced short—*atta*) is much more difficult to elucidate, because it is restricted to the language of philosophy, principally metaphysics. In that sense, it commonly refers to the "soul." It can also mean "individuality" or even the entire "body-soul unit." At times, it is also translated as "self." This philosophical usage is clearly different from the everyday usage. But it is not impossible that there is a link between the two, and that the philosophical sense is really an extension of the everyday sense of "oneself" or "one's own" to the sphere of philosophy. After all, the "soul" is, for those who believe in it, the only thing that is truly "one's own." So is one's individuality, or even one's body-soul unit.

But the real complexity of this second usage comes from the fact that the word "soul" (and to some extent even the word "self") is one that, in any language, falls into the category of abstract words. Unlike a term such as "apple" or "mango," it does not refer to a concrete object that can be seen or touched. About the meaning of such sensorially verifiable words there need not be any misunderstanding between any two users of it. But the word "soul," as also other words of the same category—such as God, gods, devil, heaven, hell—are different. Such words convey only what they are made to convey. And so, in different parts of the world, or different periods of history, or different schools of philosophy, they are used, or have been used, differently. Such words remain by their very nature vague, ambiguous, elastic.

There is no need for us to go more into detail about the variety of senses in which the word *atta* could be used. What has been said is sufficient to show that the possibility of diverse interpretations is something intrinsic to it. And so, it should not be cause for surprise if its negative form—*anatta*—has given rise to different interpretations, and has been instrumental in the development of distinct philosophical systems. Among these, two are particularly noteworthy.

One is the metaphysical theory that human beings have no soul—a theory strongly advocated by the Theravada school of Buddhism. According to that theory, the physical body and its component parts may be real, but there is no soul that links the parts together, nor is there anything beneath them that can be said to survive. From moment to moment the human being is a different individual.

The other is the theory that everything is empty. This theory is common to practically all the schools of the Mahayana group, and very particularly to the school known as Madhyamika. According to to this theory, human beings have neither souls nor bodies. Paradoxical as it may sound, emptiness (*sunyata*) is the greater reality behind human beings and even the universe itself.

Anyone studying the different schools of Buddhist thought should be ready to accept those theories as characteristic of the particular schools. Taken in their context, those interpretations of *anatta* could have great value.

That does not, of course, mean that those interpretations are necessarily in harmony with the original teachings of Gautama. As anyone with an elementary knowledge of the history and evolution of religions will grant, simple assertions made by religious founders and recorded in sacred books have often undergone such divergent interpretations at the hands of later preachers, reformers, and commentators as to beget different schools of thought and even completely different sects or denominations. A student of the history of Judaism or Christianity should be especially ready to concede that fact.

It is, however, somewhat unfortunate that Jewish and Christian students of Buddhism have up to now been exposed almost exclusively to interpretations of Buddhism made by adherents of different schools, rather than to the original teachings of Gautama. Quite naturally, it is only those interpretations that they have tried to assimilate and come to grips with. Two theories, which are aspects of these interpretations, have received particular attention from Jews and Christians. One is the "no-soul" theory and the other the "no-individuality" theory. It is therefore necessary that a word be said about those theories before the original sense of the term *anatta* is investigated.

Anatta as No-soul

According to a belief common to Christians, many Jews, and other Westerners, a human being is composed of a mortal body and an immortal soul. This Judeo-Christian Western belief originally came from classical Greek philosophy and then appeared in the first-century B.C.E. book of *Wisdom* of the Catholic canon of the Old Testament. It was subsequently adopted by Christian theology.

76

Such a belief will of course run contrary to an interpretation of *anatta* as "no-soul."

Some Christian scholars of Buddhism, motivated by the desire to bring the two religions closer to each other, have tried to show that belief in an immortal soul is not so intrinsically Christian as is generally believed. One such Protestant scholar of repute was Rev. Dr. Lynn de Silva. He wrote:

> The idea of an immortal soul is certainly a firmly established traditional belief of Christians, but it is a belief that has entered Christian thinking through the influence of Greek Philosophy and is altogether alien to what the Bible teaches about the nature and destiny of man.... It can be confidently said that in the Bible, there is no notion of an immortal soul existing independently as an eternal, immutable, and perdurable entity, which inhabits the body and escapes it at death. It is this notion that Buddhism rejects in no uncertain terms, and on this point, there is a fundamental agreement between Buddhism and biblical theology, so much so that it is possible to state the biblical view of man making use of Buddhist categories of thought [Silva, 9-10].

This, no doubt, is a truth that is very enlightening, and the intention behind its presentation is certainly admirable. In its light, a Christian should have no difficulty in subscribing to the Theravada version of *anatta*, which is that of "no-soul." But the question is: Does such a conclusion bring a Christian closer to Gautama's idea of the "no-self"? Does the Theravada interpretation adequately represent the original thought of Gautama?[4]

It must be stressed here that the Greek concept of soul has nothing to do with Gautama's concept of *atta* or *anatta*. There are many commonsense arguments against such an equation. First, the Indian theory, as discussed earlier, is not an attempt to explain the composition of the human being ontologically, as the Greek theory

77

is. It is an attempt to explain the appetitive or emotional nature of the human being in its sensations and sense perceptions. It tries to show how a human being in its act of knowledge invariably becomes a victim of *maya* or illusion.

Secondly, as with the words *anicca* and *dukkha*, Gautama used the word *anatta* to describe a low form of life, not life in its generality. Gautama believed that life could be lived at one of two levels. Of these one was ignoble and worthless, the other noble and profitable. Technically, one was called *samsara* and the other *nibbana*. It was the first, and the first alone, that was described as *anicca, dukkha*, and *anatta*. If *anatta* meant "no-soul," it would not have been restricted to the first alone.

Thirdly, if *anatta* meant no-soul, and consequently non-immortal, then after the word *anicca* the word *anatta* was redundant. It had nothing new to add. *Anicca* means "nonpermanent" or "impermanent." The term "impermanent" contains within it all that is intended by the term "non-immortal."

Finally, if we take into account Buddhism in its popular Theravada form, the notion of "non-immortality" implied by *anatta* is not reconcilable (unless a certain hairsplitting be resorted to) with the doctrine of rebirth. In popular Theravada Buddhism, rebirth is taken in a physical sense, and stands for physical survival after death. Whether with a soul or without a soul, if an individual survives death, then there is immortality in one form or another.

Many reasons such as these make it clear that when he spoke of *anatta*, Gautama could not have been referring to the problem of either mortality or immortality. That problem was entirely out of his concern. As a matter of fact, he always kept aloof from such purely abstract and speculative questions. Therefore, it is wrong to imagine that, simply by denying the immortality of the soul, one would come closer to Gautama's teaching on *anatta*; or vice versa, that by affirming it, one would be receding from it.

Happily, in this regard, it is to be noted today that there are Theravada thinkers who are seriously beginning to question whether their "no-soul" doctrine represents the authentic "no-self" concept of Gautama (see Sumangala Thera, 113 -27).

Anatta as No-individuality

Just as students of Buddhism from a Judeo-Christian Western background may have a problem with the concept of soul, so too with the concept of individuality. Individuality is one sense in which the term "self" (attributable to the term *atta*) can be taken. An individual's individuality is a reality to which great importance is attached in the Judeo-Christian Western tradition. In modern psychology, too, it is given an important place. Could Gautama's doctrine of *anatta* have implied a denial of the reality of an individual's individuality?

In day-to-day life, any ordinary person has to distinguish individuals from one another, and refer to them in contradistinction from another. That is why one speaks of an "I," "you," "he," or a "myself," "yourself," "himself." Whether we believe in immortal souls or not, it is self-evident that distinct and separate individuals exist in our society.

The pure fact of distinctness, however, is not all that makes up an individual. A tree, though distinct from another tree, is not an individual. Individuals are those who are endowed with consciousness. They can reflect on themselves as on others. They are subjects who think, judge, decide. They accept responsibility for their actions. They can, on the basis of their actions, be praised or blamed, rewarded or punished. Individuals and individuality are an objective reality, not an illusion.

By his doctrine of no-self Gautama could not have denied the existence of individuals as distinct from one another. He used the words "I," "you," "he," and "she." He spoke of reward and punishment. So, it is not individuality or responsibility that he wanted denied by his doctrine of no-self.

The Sermon on No-self Behavior

Once our minds are clear as to what Gautama could not have implied by the term *anatta*, we can direct our attention to what he really implied. For that we have to scrutinize his basic sermon on the subject, the "Sermon on the *Anatta* Characteristics" (Anatta Lakkhana Sutta). As any sect or school of Buddhism will have to grant, this is the sermon that has to be considered the most authoritative text on the topic.

This is such an important sermon that it can easily be considered a corollary to Gautama's sermon on the Four Noble Truths. It can even be taken as a direct continuation of the sermon on the Four Noble Truths for the simple reason that it was delivered almost immediately afterward and to the same group of five ascetics.

Quite obviously, like most old texts that have, in the course of transmission through centuries, lost their pristine clarity and easy readability, this text too demands of the reader a close analytical attentiveness, if the authentic sense is not to be missed. Readers interested in retrieving the original sense should make a special effort to find the thread of thought that runs through the entire sermon and, as it were, beneath the words. They should not be satisfied with isolated ideas contained in sentences or parts of sentences simply because they are easier to understand. Otherwise there is a real danger of being led to take statements out of their context and construe them to suit preconceived ideas. As a matter of fact, there are writers who have used phrases from this very text to show that what Gautama has taught is a doctrine of no-soul or no-individuality.

The text of the sermon is given below. It consists of four paragraphs, here marked a, b, c, d. The first half of the sermon, consisting of paragraphs a and b, shows why the life of the Five

Aggregates is not suitable to be identified as one's real "self," and why it has to be described as *anatta, anicca, dukkha* (*anatta* is here named first). The second half of the sermon, consisting of paragraphs c and d, points out what the attitude of noble disciples toward such a life should be. They are to disdain it and emancipate themselves from it:

(a) The body, O bhikkhus, is not one's own (*anatta*). If O bhikkhus, this were one's own, then this body should not be a source of affliction, and one should be able to demand: "Let this body be thus, let this body not be thus." But inasmuch as the body is not one's own, it is a source of affliction, and one cannot demand: Let this body be thus, let this body not be thus.

The feelings, O bhikkhus, ... [In like manner, each of the other four aggregates—namely, feelings, perception, emotional reactions, and consciousness—are then taken up and the same argument in the same verbal form is repeated.]

(b) What think you, O bhikkhus, is this body permanent or impermanent? Impermanent (*anicca*), Lord. Is that which is impermanent, happy or sorrowful? It is sorrowful (*dukkha*), Lord.
Is it justifiable then to think of that which is not under one's control, not permanent, and sorrowful as one's own, saying "This is mine," "This am I," "This is myself"? Certainly not, Lord.

[The same argument is then repeated with respect to the other four aggregates, in the same verbal form.]

(c) Then O bhikkhus, all body, whether past or present or future, personal or external, coarse or subtle, low or high, far or near, should be understood by right knowledge in its real nature: "This is not mine," "This am I not," "These are not myself."

[The same statement is then repeated in the same verbal form with respect to the other four aggregates.]

(d) The learned noble disciple who sees thus, develops a disdain for the body, for feelings, for perceptions, for emotional reactions, for consciousness. Through this disdain, he gets detached from them. Through detachment, he becomes an emancipated being. Then dawns on him the knowledge: "Emancipated am I." He understands that rebirth is ended, pure life has been won. This sad state of life will never recur again [MV, I, 6, 38-47].

This sermon takes as its basis the reality known as the Five Aggregates—namely, body, feelings, perceptions, emotional reactions, and consciousness. The text takes them one by one, and the whole argumentation of the sermon is built on what is said of each of them. To each of them is attributed the epithets *anicca, dukkha, anatta*.

The doctrine of the Five Aggregates, as is well known, is not an invention of Gautama. He used it exactly as it was commonly understood in the Indian society of his day. If therefore, we are to grasp what Gautama is saying here, we have to have a clear vision of the function and purpose of the Indian theory of the Five Aggregates. As has often happened, a wrong understanding of it can lead to wrong interpretations.

As explained earlier, the theory of the Five Aggregates, known also as the Name-Form (*nama rupa*) theory, was meant to serve one particular purpose. It was meant to underline and explain the emotion-rooted, emotion-filled, emotion-dominated form of life of the majority of human beings. In other words, it explained the behavior of human beings on the plane known as *samsara*, or the cycle of birth and rebirth. It did not undertake to analyze the physical structure of the human being, as did, for instance, the Greek matter-form or body-soul theory. Not to see that fact would be a gross mistake. The life of the Five Aggregates was a state from which an escape was possible. *Nibbana* was the name of the state of life of the individual who had found emancipation from it. In the day-to-day life of *nibbana*, human beings were governed by reason, not by emotion.

With this basic fact kept in mind, we should have no difficulty in reading this sermon perspicaciously and learning from it the answers to the questions with which we were confronted at the start. We turned to this sermon to find the answer to two questions: (a) What is the meaning of the word *anatta* and in what sense did Gautama use it in the *anicca-dukkha-anatta* formula? (b) Did Gautama preach a doctrine of "no-self"? If so, what is the exact nature and content of that doctrine?
Anatta: Meaning of the Term

In the first paragraph, which is devoted exclusively to an analysis of the term *anatta*, Gautama takes the emotion-dominated life of the Five Aggregates and asks whether such a life (i.e., body, feelings, emotional reactions, etc.) should ever be considered "one's own," or taken as "one's real self"? Gautama's view is that it should not be so considered; and he gives the reason for it.

Such a life, being under the sway of the emotions instead of under the control of reason, is "not under one's control." No one can simply dictate: "Let me be so, let me not be so." In other words, according to Gautama, persons under the sway of the emotions, are not their own masters. They are much more prisoners of their emotions. They do not enjoy any power of self-determination. It is that state of slavishness that Gautama pinpoints by the term *anatta*. Literally it means "not one's own." If we take it along with its underlying reason, it means: "not one's own, because not under one's control."

83

To put it differently, what Gautama is underlining here by the use of the term *anatta* is the autonomy-less-ness of an emotion-dominated life. It is difficult for us to find a single adequate English word for the Pali word *anatta*. But we could say that a term such as "autonomy-less" or "non-autonomous" would come very close to it.

Anyone who doubts the validity of the above interpretation of *anatta* will do well to read a second sermon which, though very much the same in pattern, is even clearer. It is the "Cula Saccaka Sutta" (*Mahayamaka Vagga*, 5), which was delivered not to his followers but an adversary. Aggisevana, a member of another religious organization, had heard that Gautama was propounding a doctrine called *anatta*, and that he was denying the "self" (or the "one's own-ness") of the Five Aggregates. With the intention of challenging this doctrine, he visited Gautama and said:

> "Teacher, Gautama, I affirm without hesitation that this body (*rupa*) of mine is my 'self' (my own). That my feeling (*vedana*), my perception (*sañña*), my emotional reactions (*samkhara*), my consciousness (*viññana*) are my 'self' (my own)."

> "Well then, Aggisevana, let me ask you this. Think well and answer me.... Could a noble anointed king, such as for instance, King Pasenadi of Kosala, or King Ajatasattu of Magadha be taken as having power within his territory if he was not capable of putting to death one deserving of death, of punishing one deserving of punishment, of banishing one deserving of banishment?"

> "Teacher, Gautama, surely a king such as King Pasenadi or King Ajatasattu will have such power. Even ordinary chieftains have such power, and so, how much more power will such kings have?"

84

"What then do you think about this? When you say, 'this body is my "self" (my own),' can you say you have power over this body of yours, and can you order it about saying 'Let my body be this, let my body be that.' Or when you say that feeling is my own... perception is my own... emotional reactions are my own ... consciousness is my own... can you say you have power over any of these? Can you order them saying, 'Let me be so, let me not be so.' If not, how can you consider yourself your own master?"

Gautama's reply to Aggisevana, restricted here to an illustration, shows clearly why Gautama taught that the "self" of the Five Aggregates is not a real "self." A king who has no authority over his subjects, and so no control over his country, cannot call that country really his. So is it with the "self." A "self" that is not under one's control is not one's own.

With an assertion so clear as that coming from the mouth of Gautama himself, there can be no room for doubt that the original sense of the word *anatta* was a simple one. It meant "not one's own." But he attached a very insightful nuance to it: "not one's own because not under one's control."

The False Self

Nevertheless, if we, without restricting ourselves to the single word *anatta*, take into account the whole sermon and particularly what it says about the Five Aggregates, will be obliged to admit that there is contained in it a strong denunciation by Gautama of a "self" of a particular form. The term "self," as such, is not found in the text of the sermon, but it is a term by which the expression "Five Aggregates" can be rendered. However ephemeral its meanings may seem to be, "self" is still the term that is commonly used to describe that element which makes an individual an individual. It makes "me" a "myself," "him" a "himself," and "her" a "herself." Because each person can have his or her own "self," it is clear that there can be a variety of forms of the "self." Gautama took all those individual forms of the "self" and divided them into two main categories.

One category he called the "self" of the Five Aggregates. It is that form of the "self" that he referred to also by the term *samsara* (rebirth). He derogatorily described the *samsara*, or the Five-Aggregate form of human behavior, as *anicca, dukkha, anatta*, that is, as transient, sorrowful, and non-autonomous.

That original meaning of the term "Five Aggregates" was ignored by later commentators. That is an important point to be kept in mind when the Theravada or the Mahayana theories of the "self" are studied. Later commentators took the term to mean not just a pattern of behavior but the physical entity as such. The term *anatta* was applied to this interpretation of the Five Aggregates. Thereafter, depending on the sense attributed to the term *anatta*, the human being came to be considered as an entity either without a soul or without any reality.

Such an interpretation does not tally either with the purpose with which Gautama preached the sermon or with what is clearly asserted in the concluding part of the sermon. Gautama's aim in preaching the sermon was to make his listeners become disgusted with the low, childish form of behavior that most people generally pursued, and thereafter to make them give it up in favor of an adult form of behavior that he considered more noble and more in keeping with human dignity. It was the latter that he called the "emancipated life." The joyful exclamation "Emancipated am I" that he put into the mouth of the liberated disciples, and which appears at the very end of the sermon, makes that very clear: "Emancipated am I; rebirth (*samsara*) is ended; pure life has been won. This sad state of life will never recur.

That final statement of the sermon does not leave any room for doubt as to the correct sense in which the terms "Five Aggregates" has to be taken. The emancipation that Gautama envisaged was not a matter of a life that follows death. It was emancipation from a false set of values to be given up straightaway. The post-*samsara* reality itself was a noble form of human behavior to be practiced here and now.

Introspection is needed to understand the "self" that Gautama considered as ignoble, as unrealistic, and as to be discarded. That "self" cannot be seen or touched. It can only be hinted at. To understand this, one has to look inside oneself and not outside oneself. When it is discovered, it will be seen for what in reality it is, a "no-self." It is just a mirage or an illusion, entirely self-created. But, amazingly, even though only an illusion, it is something that everybody almost madly holds on to.

It is this "self" that is behind the feeling of "self-importance." It is the "ego" behind "egoism." It is the individual behind (not individuality but) individualism.

For Gautama, there was nothing so detrimental and so harmful to a human being's achievement of true nobility as the blind adherence to the "self" that he termed the "Five Aggregates." He spoke against it so vehemently and so incessantly that without any hesitation we have to say that his religious philosophy was basically one of "no-self" or "anti-self." The adherence to the belief in this false form of "self" was, according to him, what people had invariably to be liberated from if their lives were ever to become joyful, noble, and meaningful.

Universal Import of the Doctrine of the No-self

As in the time of Gautama, today too, every human being believes in a great false "I." Probably no modern writer has expressed so bluntly this false assumption of every person as did Kierkegaard when he said, "In the secret bottom of his heart, each human being thinks that he is at the center of the world." Anyone sincere enough to look into their inner thoughts at any given moment will see how true this statement is.

The best moment to catch a glimpse of this emotional monster in humans that Gautama called the "self" is when it is in action. One such moment is when two individuals who are equals, such as co-workers or neighbors, encounter one another. The one has only to speak of having obtained a better job, a new car, or a promotion and the "self" in the other begins to peer out draped in the cloak of jealousy, the most common and most dreadful of human vices. Jealousy may start simply as a feeling of uneasiness within the heart of an individual, but it soon develops into a violent hatred. At times, this hatred even takes on murderous proportions.

This "self" has such a conviction of its superiority that all its equals appear to it as competitors. Before an equal it invariably tells itself, "I am the greatest. My competitor challenges my greatness. My competitor is my enemy. I must destroy competitors, make myself greater."

Jealousy is so much a part of human nature that, however well-intentioned a person may be, it is impossible not to experience some jealousy when one sees some good happening to another. ("Another" here means an equal and one who is not psychologically a part of one's life, such as a brother or sister, father or mother.) The *very first reaction* is necessarily one of jealousy. Even religious persons, unless they be an *arahat, zaddik*, or saint, can act religiously and without jealousy only in the *second thought*, not the first. This is a strange human phenomenon that a Christian would explain as derived from original sin or fallen nature, a Jew by *yetzer ha ra* or evil impulse, and a Buddhist as the samsaric state of *dukkha*.

Another moment at which the "self" shows its face clearly is when it is covetous. Persons cannot but covet something that their senses portray to them as pleasing. Covetousness has necessarily to be a human being's first reaction. It is only in the *second thought* that even a religious person can view a pleasurable object with detachment and rationality.

The "self" becomes equally visible in the repeated efforts of an individual to "show off" or "put on a front." The "self" wants its bearer to appear before others as someone more than he or she in reality is. One indication of this tendency is the extravagant use of cosmetics. Another is the craze for "fashion" in dress. We should not be misled into believing that the reason behind "make up" and "fashion" is solely the desire to appear pleasant or beautiful before others. Such an intention would be praiseworthy. The hidden reason is rather to be more than one truly is, to be the person whom one secretly thinks of as a great person; often it is based on a desire to imitate a popular celebrity.

No one understands this behavior of the "self" in humanity and exploits it so cleverly to their personal advantage as the advertisers of commercial products. However, poor be the quality of the soap or the toothpaste to be sold, the advertisement has only to say that this movie star or that sports hero uses it, and the article sells.

Pretense or role-playing is not a game restricted to secular society. Religious persons, too, often indulge in it. Many, for instance, like to "play the saint." They want to appear holy, as persons who give alms, who pray, who fast. One who clearly recognized this game was Jesus. He saw certain hypocrites playing it with great dexterity and he warned his disciples against following such behavior:

> Be on your guard against performing religious actions for people to see.... When you give alms for example, do not blow a horn before you in synagogues and streets like hypocrites, looking for applause. You can be sure of this much. They are already repaid. [Note, Jesus can be sarcastic.] In giving alms, you are not to let your left hand know what your right hand is doing. Keep your deeds of mercy secret and your Father who sees in secret will repay you.
>
> When you are praying, do not behave like the hypocrites who love to pray and stand in

synagogues or on street corners in order to be noticed. I give you my word, they are repaid. When you pray go to your room, close your door and pray to your Father, in secret.

When you fast, you are not to look glum as the hypocrites do. They change the appearance of their faces so that others may see they are fasting. . . . When you fast see to it that you groom your hair and wash your face; in that way, no one can see you are fasting except your Father who is hidden [Matt. 6:16-18].

The ancient Rabbis of the Talmud also mercilessly pilloried hypocritical Pharisees when they listed seven classes of Pharisees, only the last two of which were pronounced authentic:

1. The "Shoulder" Pharisee, who ostentatiously carries his good deeds on the shoulder to be seen by all.
2. The "Wait-A-While" Pharisee, who when someone needs him says, "Wait until I have done this good deed."
3. The "Reckoning" or "Book-keeping" Pharisee, who calculates virtue against vice. This Pharisee may sin deliberately and then attempt to cross off the fault by adding a good deed to his list.
4. The "Bruised" Pharisee, who breaks his head against a wall to avoid looking at a woman or is so ostentatious in his "humility" that he keeps shuffling his feet together and wounding them.
5. The "Pestle" Pharisee, whose head is bent in sham humility like a pestle in a mortar.
6. The "God-fearing Pharisee," who is like Job.
7. The "Pharisee of Love," who is like Abraham [Berachoth 9:7; Sotah 5:7; (Fisher, 38f.)].

Just as in Jesus', the Talmudists', or Gautama's day, hypocrisy, or the belief in a false "self," prevents persons today from discovering true holiness, personality, and adulthood. The few illustrations given above should be enough to show how true to life Gautama's analysis of humanity and his psychology are.

All that Gautama has done in his no-self (*anatta*) doctrine is to show what true personality is and what it is not. It is not easy for anyone to describe human maturity. It can be done only by contrasting it with childish behavior. Gautama has pointed to the place where persons mistakenly look for greatness to say that true human greatness is not there. True greatness is not where reason is enslaved by the emotions, where the highest value is that of sense-pleasure, or where the pattern of life is one of greed, pride, or self-delusion (*raga, dosa, moha*).

To the extent that we understand the no-self doctrine of Gautama, to that extent we can say we have grasped the meaning of Right Understanding. The goal of Right Understanding is nothing but an objective understanding of the reality of one's own life. Life, as lived at a purely emotional level, is *anicca, dukkha, anatta*. It is transient, sorrowful, autonomy-less.

Once we understand that, it is not difficult for us to realize, what true religion is for Gautama. For him, religion is reality. To be religious is to be rational. To be a religious person is to be a mature adult.

Chapter Ten

Right Thought, Right Speech, Right Action

The second, third, and fourth steps of the Eightfold Path are Right Thought, Right Speech, and Right Action, respectively. Inasmuch as thought, speech, and action are generally considered to be intrinsically connected in a given person, it is justifiable to treat these three steps together. Also, Western students would already have some idea of the behavior patterns implied by these steps and would be able to understand them without further explanation, and so they are treated here in summary form in one chapter.

Right Thoughts

Immediately after Right Understanding, the first step of the Eightfold Path, Gautama listed Right Thought. Right Thought is not the same as Right Understanding, but the one flows from the other. Right Understanding is a vision of reality, but Right Thoughts are inner yearnings, aspirations, and wishes. One can have right yearnings only if one has a right vision.
Gautama detailed Right Thought as:

1. thoughts of renunciation,
2. thoughts of good will,
3. thoughts of non-harming or compassion (MN, I, 114, Sutta 19).

They are the opposite of the thoughts that are more normal and typical of the human mind, which are:

1. thoughts of sense-desire,
2. thoughts of ill will,

3. thoughts of harm or violence (ibid.).

Westerners today recognize the place of right thought in the development of an individual's personality. One Western book that clearly suggests the effect of thought on a person's behavior is Dr. Norman Vincent Peale's *The Power of Positive Thinking*, a book that has had a character-transforming effect on a large sector of American society. In it he says:

> As you think, so shall you be. So, flush out all old, tired, worn out thoughts. Fill your mind with fresh, new, creative thoughts of faith, love, and goodness. By this process, you can almost re-make your life.... You can think your way to failure and unhappiness; but also, you can think your way to success and happiness. The world in which you live is not primarily determined by outward conditions and circumstances, but by thoughts that habitually occupy your mind. Remember the wise words of Marcus Aurelius... who said, "A man's life is what thoughts make of it" [Peale, 201-4].

When we notice the position Gautama has given to Right Thought, we have to say that Gautama was a proponent of "positive thinking" twenty-five hundred years ago. Because he was aware of the power of thought on life, he suggested to his disciples that they always fill their minds with feelings of detachment, good will, and compassion, and erase thoughts of sense-desire, ill will, and violence.

Renunciation. The first type of good thought that Gautama wished to see developed is that of renunciation. Renunciation is a basic concept in all religions, although it has at times been understood in a purely physical sense as a withdrawal into the wilderness. The monk and the nun are generally thought of as persons who renounce the world. But renunciation is not restricted to the monastery or the convent. As Gautama says: "Because he has put aside evil, he is called a *Brahmin* [priest]. Because he lives in serenity, he is called a *Samana* [recluse]. Because he puts away his impurities, he is called a *Pabbajjita* [anchorite]" (*Dhammapada*, chap. 26, 6).

The "world" that is to be given up, thus, is not the physical world composed of plants, animals, and human beings, but the mental world founded on desire and greed. Renunciation is a transition from the *spirit of worldliness* to the *spirit of unworldliness*. One may well remain in the world (i.e., secular society) and yet practice renunciation. Renunciation taken at depth is simply self-mastery.

Good will. Thoughts of good will toward others is the second type of thought with which Gautama wanted his disciples to fill their minds. Buddhism has been described at times as a negative religion, insisting only on self-control, but this is because many have failed to realize the importance given by Gautama to the diffusion of thoughts of good will. According to Gautama (as will be explained in chap. 14), every person should project thoughts of friendliness toward others and even toward those who are not friends.

Buddhism, it is true, does not stress the performance of acts of charity as do Judaism, Christianity, and Islam. But persons who fill their minds with friendly thoughts when alone cannot fail to put those thoughts into action when they are with others.

Compassion. Compassion is a difficult virtue to practice and probably the virtue that the modern world most needs. Compassion is the quality that arouses tender feelings in an individual at the sight of another's suffering. Jesus spoke of it through his parable on Dives and Lazarus (Luke 16:19-3 1). Quite indifferent to the sufferings of Lazarus, Dives was able to continue living a life of luxury; for Jesus, such indifference was an unpardonable crime.

It is not only in the ancient Hebrew Bible that the injunction to "love your neighbor as yourself" is found (Lev. 19:18). It is also in many of the Jewish writings two hundred years before the time of Jesus: "Love the Lord in your whole life and one another with a sincere heart" (*Testament of Daniel*, 5:3); "Love the Lord and the neighbor" (*Testament of Issachar*, 5:2); "And he commanded them to keep to the way of God, do justice, and everyone love his neighbor" (*Jubilees*, 20:9); "Love one another, my sons, as brothers, as one loves oneself.... You should love one another as yourselves" (*Jubilees*, 36:4-6).

Compassion is a virtue that is very important to Buddhism. In Mahayana Buddhism, it is conidered the central virtue. As Piyadassi Thera says: "If you remove *karuna* (compassion) from the teachings of the Buddha you remove the heart of Buddhism, for, all virtues, all goodness, and righteousness have *karuna* as their basis, as their matrix" (Piyadassi Thera, 120).

Taken together, the three right thoughts of detachment, of good will, and of compassion illustrate that what Gautama is promoting through Right Thoughts is an attitude of control toward oneself and of benevolence toward others.

Right Speech

As persons think, so will they speak. Therefore, Right Speech necessarily follows Right Thought. Right Speech is also a virtue that Jesus insisted on. He said that truly religious persons are so truthful that they do not need to have recourse to an oath to confirm that they are telling the truth:

> You have learned how it was said to our ancestors "you must not break your oath, but must fulfil your oaths made before the Lord." And I say to you ... all you need to say is "yes" if you mean "yes" and "no" if you mean "no" [Matt. 5:33-37].

In the Jewish midrash on Ruth 3:18 Rabbi Huna said: "The 'yes' of a just person is a 'yes,' and the 'no' of a just person is a 'no'" (Billerbeck, I, 336).

In this teaching on Right Speech, Gautama has drawn attention to four types of wrong speech that should be avoided by the truly mature person:

1. falsehood,
2. slander,
3. harsh words,
4. gossip (MN, 111, 252).

Falsehood. Truthfulness is a very difficult virtue to practice. The safeguarding of objectivity is often not the primary concern of persons when they have something to say. What they say has to safeguard fame and reputation. It has to help them reap benefits and favors from others. It must make their business prosper. They are concerned about the judgment of political and religious superiors. Objectivity in speech, therefore, is not easy, which is why truthfulness is possible only to one who truly possesses an adult and liberated mind.

Gautama's advice to his own son Rahula, who had become a monk, shows the importance he attached to truthfulness:

> Rahula, void and empty is the reclusion of those who are not ashamed to lie. Even so, Rahula, of anyone who is not ashamed to lie, I say there is no evil that he cannot do. Wherefore, Rahula, thus indeed should you train yourself: "Not even for fun will I tell a lie" [MN, I, 414, Sutta 61].

Slander. Slander here refers to calumny and detraction. The Pali word for it, *pisuna vaca*, means "breaking fellowship." In Sanskrit poetry, a backbiter is compared to a mosquito who, though small, is noxious. It comes, sings, settles on an individual, draws blood and, at times, imparts malaria. Slander can also be compared to a murderer's knife, for it is a tool widely used in the killing of reputations.

Harsh words. Mature adults do not resort to harsh words to enforce expected performance. Rather they put all their confidence in gentleness. They know that a gentle word can melt the hardest heart, whereas a harsh word can cause agony.

Today, the science of business administration has discovered the selling power hidden within kind words. Salespersons are advised: be courteous. But the courtesy of noble persons is not prompted by the profit motive. It is their benevolence and acceptance of everyone as a friend that inspires them to be courteous.

Gossip. Mature adults do not engage in frivolous or meaningless talk. They say nothing that is not in some way beneficial to the one who listens. They never disparage others. They follow in this the teaching of the *Dhammapada*: "Better than a thousand sentences is one sensible phrase, on hearing which one becomes peaceful" (*Dhammapada*, chap. 8, 1).

Gautama insisted on good speech because he knew what its power was in the transformation of individuals and of society. On one occasion, he advised:

> The good say: Noble speech is apt. Therefore, express reality, not non-reality. Say what is pleasant, not what is unpleasant. Speak what is true, not lies. Speak only words that do not bring remorse, nor hurt another. That is good speech indeed [*Suttanipata*, Subhasita Sutta].

Right Action

The fourth step of the Eightfold Path is Right Action. The term "action" here is broadly used and includes three different aspects of human conduct:

refraining from killing,
refraining from stealing,

refraining from wrong sexual behavior (MN, III, 252, Sutta 141).

Jews and Christians are familiar with these requirements of good character; they are found in the Ten Commandments. Five commandments refer to these three character traits:

Fifth Commandment: Do not kill.
Seventh Commandment: Do not steal.
Tenth Commandment: Do not even covet the neighbor's goods.
Sixth Commandment: Do not commit adultery.
Ninth Commandment: Do not even covet the neighbor's wife.

These three elements of right action are so fundamental to the well-being and good order of society that they are found not only in the ethical codes of religions but also in the penal codes of civil society. As a result, there are many who observe them solely for fear of punishment by civil authorities. Truly ethical persons follow them voluntarily, without any such fear. They do so from a sense of personal obligation to the family of humankind of which they consider themselves integral parts.

Refraining from killing. We commonly understand killing to be the taking of an individual's life —murder. It is in that sense that penal codes define it, but a religious person, whether Buddhist, Christian, or Jewish, understands this principle in a broader sense as "reverence for life."

Truly mature persons not only refrain from taking life, they also do everything they can to preserve life. They do their best to see that their neighbor, whether near or far, is enabled to live in a dignified way with peace of mind and economic security.

The Buddhist precept, however, also demands the protection of animals. Because of this dimension, many a modern Buddhist is unable to justify the Judeo-Christian attitude toward animals. Among Jews and Christians, the raising of animals for food is not considered unlawful. This diversity in the Buddhist and Judeo-

Christian approach to the life of animals is a delicate point that needs to be carefully scrutinized for better understanding among the three religions.

Cruelty to animals—and the wanton destruction of trees and vegetation is, from a Judeo-Christian point of view, incorrect. All animals and vegetative life are the product of God's creation, and to destroy them *without a justifiable reason* is contrary to God's purposes.

Nevertheless, the natural order of the universe is such that, for the justifiable reasons of self-preservation and nutrition, the killing of animals is held to be permissible. In the struggle for continued existence, a tiger may eat a monkey, a lizard may eat a fly, a bigger fish may eat a smaller one. From the point of view of human sentiment and emotion, this may appear to be cruel, but life itself requires that sentiment be subject to reason.

Gautama himself, in his day, had to face the conflict between sentiment and reason in this field. Some of his followers tried to bring pressure upon him to prohibit the use of meat by his disciples. He understood the sentiment and the emotional feeling that prompted this suggestion. He also saw the argument of reason that the eating of meat was, in large part, a necessity. In seeking a compromise between sentiment and reason, he ordained that meat be eaten by monks only on two conditions: that they have not seen the killing, and that the animals have not been killed exclusively for their sake. By this solution, he saved reason without unduly damaging sentiment (VP/MV, 238, chap. 6, 31-34).

Stealing. Taking what belongs to another is stealing. This is an action that can be perpetrated in many more subtle ways than just by burglaries or highway robberies. Inasmuch as the implications of the Buddhist precept are not so different from those of the Judeo-Christian precept, no special elaboration on it is necessary here.

Wrong Sexual Behavior. It would be an error to think that simply because monastic life is a basic element of Theravada Buddhism that the doctrine of Right Action calls for abstinence from sex. The scriptures clearly show that the laity formed as great a part of the disciples of Gautama as did the monks. Lay followers were referred to as *gihi kamabhogino*, "laymen enjoying the pleasures of the senses" (MN, I, 490), and this expression is not used in a derogatory or condemnatory manner. For Gautama, there was a right enjoyment of sense-pleasure as well as an abuse of it. Total abstinence is the sole remedy for sexual abuse.

Gautama, however, did not underestimate the effort required in maintaining a right balance in a person's sex life. The philosophy of Gautama recognizes that sex is the strongest impulse in humans, and that its right use calls for an equally strong self-control. The opening discourse in the *Anguttara Nikaya* makes it very explicit:

> Monks, I know not of any other single form (or sound, or smell or flavor, or touch) by which a man's heart is attracted as it is by that of a woman. Monks, a woman's form, sound, smell, flavor, touch, fill a man's mind.

> Monks, I know not any other single form, sound, smell, flavor, and touch by which a woman's heart is attracted as it is by the form, sound, smell, flavor, and touch of a man. Monks, a woman's mind is filled with these things.

Chastity, however, whether in its marital form or in its celibate form, is primarily a matter of mental attitude or depth. No one can be chaste in action without also being chaste in mind, although one can be celibate in body without being chaste in mind. This is strikingly illustrated by a story of Zen Buddhism.

Two monks, traveling together, approached a stream whose water was at high level. A young girl also wanting to cross the river hesitated to venture into the water for fear of the strong current.

One of the monks, observing her helplessness, offered to come to her aid. He took her into his arms, carried her across the stream, and left her on the shore.

The two monks continued their journey. As they came to the end of the journey, the other monk burst out with an observation he could no longer keep to himself. "Venerable Sir, I have all this time been worried. I have been wondering whether you as a celibate did the right thing by carrying that young girl across the river in your arms."

The first monk's answer was abrupt. "I carried her across and left her on the shore, but you seem to be carrying her still!" Chastity in Buddhism is a virtue based on a chaste attitude of mind, and perfect chastity becomes universal benevolence.

This spirit of universal benevolence, in Gautama's thought, should characterize human conduct in all its forms, be it in regard to life (refraining from killing), be it in regard to sexual relationships (refraining from wrong sexual behavior), or in regard to property (refraining from stealing). An attitude of such selfless benevolence causes a person's action to be Right Action.

The basis of Right Action, as also of the two other steps discussed in this chapter, Right Thoughts and Right Speech, can be said to be selfless benevolence or selflessness and benevolence.

Chapter Eleven

Right Livelihood

To those who think that Buddhism is exclusively a form of meditation or even a form of monasticism, the inclusion of Right Livelihood as one of the elements of the Eightfold Path is bound to come as a shock. "Livelihood" refers to the secular employment or profession by which lay persons earn an income to maintain themselves and their families.

Right Livelihood and Lay Spirituality

An inquirer into Buddhism cannot be criticized for thinking that Buddhism is exclusively a form of monasticism: that is the impression that one receives from reading current Buddhist scriptures. This is particularly true of the sacred scriptures pertaining to the Theravada tradition.[5]

The Theravada doctrine, as we have it today, was committed to writing a few centuries after the death of Gautama by monks, for the benefit of monks, and in monasteries. They were not written by lay persons or for lay persons. With such an origin, it is natural that the scriptures have given little prominence to the sermons that Gautama addressed to the laity. In fact, very few of Gautama's sermons addressed to laity are contained in the sacred scriptures.[6]

There is no question but that Gautama devoted an important part of his life and energy to the establishment of a monastic way of life. There is also no question but that he himself was a monk, although (and this, also, is very important to remember) of a non-ascetic and even anti-ascetic type. Nevertheless, he has nowhere presented monastic life as the only way to liberation. His inclusion of Right

Livelihood as an intrinsic element of the Eightfold Path, which, as already mentioned, belongs to his earliest traceable teachings, clearly confirms that fact.

Theravada tradition, however, has generally upheld that perfect liberation, or arahatship, was possible only in the monastic life. The monks who upheld that theory naturally restricted the meaning of Right Livelihood and defined it as something applicable only to the life of the monk.

Such an explanation distorts the original intention. It makes the inclusion of Right Livelihood in the Eightfold Path unnecessary, unrealistic, and meaningless, for the simple reason that monks were not allowed a "livelihood." The very term *bhikkhu* (literally, "mendicant"), the name that has been used from the earliest days to designate a Buddhist monk, implied that he was required to live exclusively on alms from lay supporters. To speak of "livelihood," a means of earning an income, with reference to persons living *on alms* destroys its significance.

A Theravada-Mahayana Controversy

By insisting on the original definition of Right Livelihood, we enter a sensitive area of Buddhism in its institutionalized forms. An important point of controversy that separates the Mahayana branch of Buddhism from the Theravada is exactly this issue of a lay person's access to liberation.

The Mahayana upheld that the doors of liberation were open equally to the lay person and to the monk. The Theravada, on the contrary, though not denying the theoretical possibility of a lay person's liberation, tended to affirm that in practice this was only rarely possible. The difference of approach explains the distinction of the terms Mahayana and Hinayana. *Maha-yana* means "large vehicle": it carries many—monks and laity—to liberation. *Hina-yana* means "small vehicle": it carries only a few—monks—to liberation. Hinayana was a nickname coined by the Mahayanists to designate the Theravada philosophy.

Incidentally, the greater interest currently evidenced by Western countries in Mahayana rather than in Theravada may well have its foundation here. Undoubtedly many Westerners are seeking in Buddhism a philosophy of liberation that would be applicable to their state of life as lay persons.

The difference in the Mahayana and the Theravada attitudes toward the lay person's place in religion has some parallel in Christianity in the Catholic-Protestant division. (Monasticism largely ended in Judaism with the disappearance of the Essenes from Palestinian Judaism and the Therapeutae from Hellenistic Judaism, both in the first century C.E.) Roman Catholicism, very much like Theravada Buddhism, is based on a monastic foundation functioning under the administration of an exclusively celibate clergy. Even though Roman Catholicism does not restrict salvation to the celibate, the priesthood and church administration are exclusively restricted (at least in the majority, Latin rite branch) to celibate priests, monks, and nuns. Protestantism, much like Mahayana Buddhism, is built on quite a different approach to celibacy and the priesthood. Lay persons play an essential role in the religious and organizational activities of Protestant churches.

It is not necessary to delve further into the Theravada-Mahayana controversies at this point. The specific difference referred to is, however, helpful in understanding how Right Livelihood has been integrated into the Eightfold Path.

Significance of Right Livelihood

There is something very novel and very original in the inclusion of Right Livelihood as an element of the path to liberation. The importance that Gautama thus gives to Right Livelihood provides a valuable lesson for religious persons in any period of time.

All religions in their institutionalized forms—Christianity, Judaism, Islam, Hinduism, and even modern Buddhism—often make their devotees feel that liberation or sanctification comes from one's closeness to the priest, rabbi, imam, monk, or the like. For many a religious-minded person of today, religion is primarily a participation in sacrifices, rituals, and sacraments, and for some it veers toward ethnocentrism.

Rite and ritual do have a socio-religious value within institutionalized structures, but that value is basically symbolic and educational in character. Sacrifice and sacraments are primarily a ritually dramatized expression of the selflessness, self-control, and self-denial required in ordinary life. They are thus only a means to an end. But most religions, forgetting the limited role of rite and ritual, consider worship in church or temple the decisive factor in religion, and consequently relegate marketplace religion to the periphery. This approach is harmful to the very cause of religion. The success of contemporary forms of humanism, and particularly of communism, in divorcing modern persons from religion, lies in this wrong tendency to equate ritual with religion.

Gautama's insistence on Right Livelihood is in that sense a reaction to such interpretations of religion. It is, in a way, a great blow aimed at the exaggerated exaltation of the liberative power of temple life. Liberation for him lies in the right performance of daily duties. Persons must earn their living. If that responsibility is properly exercised, they will find liberation in that very action. Work itself possesses greater humanizing power than does rite and ritual. Gautama's doctrine of Right Livelihood teaches that, for perfect humanhood, religion practiced in one's daily life is more important than church or temple rituals.

Principles of Right Livelihood

Gautama illustrated Right Livelihood by examples from the society of his time. This society of twenty-five hundred years ago consisted mainly of farmers, shepherds, and traders. As examples of livelihood to be avoided, he singled out the sale of arms and lethal weapons, the slaughter of animals and human beings, and the production of intoxicating drinks and poisons.

Examination of these three examples reveals that each of them entails a disservice to humankind involving a serious human damage of one form or another. Earning money in a field of endeavor that ultimately results in a disservice or damage to humankind is not a legitimate or liberative form of livelihood. Humans can legitimately earn money only by a service performed for another, not by an exploitation of the other.

Modern society has comfortably defined a job or profession solely as a way of earning money, which justifies any industry or trade as long as it produces income. Service is considered an accidental by-product of the job. Liberated persons, however, reverse this order. Income for them is only the consequence of a service rendered to another. For them the value of a job or profession lies not in the amount of payment attached to it, but in the value of the service or help rendered. In their scale of values benevolence comes before money. Such a view of life is possible only to those for whom livelihood is an element on the path to their own liberation.

Jesus expressed an idea that is very similar when, commenting on human anxiety over the needs of life, he said, "Seek ye first the reign of God and its righteousness, and all these things will be added on to you" (Matt. 6:33). In this context, to "seek the reign of God" is to practice the virtues of justice and charity in one's dealings with others. To such a seeker after the reign of God the needs of daily life-food, clothing, shelter-will be given.

The Rabbis of the Midrashim said almost the same thing: "'Lord of the universe, I ask for wisdom, that you give me wisdom and knowledge.' God said to him: 'Because you have asked for wisdom, in your life all things will flow from wisdom—thus wisdom and knowledge shall be given to you, and wealth and riches and honor will I give you'" (Billerbeck, I, 440).

Right Livelihood, correctly understood, reveals the principles that should guide the economic actions of individuals, groups, and nations. *"Earning without disserving,"* which is the principle behind the teaching of Right Livelihood, has a message for all humankind.

To sum up Gautama's thought using an oriental image, a responsible wage earner's activity should be very different from the behavior of the mosquito. The mosquito sucks blood from another, leaving only pain and injury. The enlightened wage earner should rather imitate the behavior of the bee. it helps each plant in the process of pollination and eventual fructification, receiving honey in return. The one who practices Right Livelihood, like the bee, has a double joy: that of a service done for humankind, and a means of personal maintenance found through that very service.

Chapter Twelve

Right Effort

The doctrine of Right Effort contains two very valuable lessons. The first, if propounded as advice, would be: strive hard to achieve life's aims. Greatness is achieved only by effort, determination, and perseverance.

The indispensability of strenuous effort is not an idea new to our contemporaries, particularly in Western society. All the progress made by the modern world is the result of effort. The progress made in the sciences, in industry, in agriculture, and particularly in the exploration of other planets would not have been possible without industriousness and sustained effort.

Against such a background, it would not be presumptuous to ask whether Right Effort of the Eightfold Path has anything to offer modern humanity. In truth, it has. The effort recommended by Gautama is aimed at a target altogether different and more elevated than that which ordinarily concerns modern humanity. Through his doctrine of Right Effort, Gautama seems to be saying: "Strive hard to be enlightened human beings, human beings who are great, not just in material riches, but in maturity."

For Gautama, the achievement of a noble character is the outcome of very strenuous and persistent effort. To become an enlightened being, a person must make a greater effort than to become a business executive, a sports celebrity, or a highly qualified academician. The resolution made by Gautama during his search for enlightenment shows the vigorous energy output that is implied in Right Effort. "Verily, let skin, sinews, and bones remain; let flesh and blood in the body dry up; yet shall there be no decrease of energy till that which is to be won by vigorous strength, energy and effort is to be attained" (MN, I, 482, Sutta 70).

The second lesson propounded by the doctrine of Right Effort relates to the precise nature of the goal to be striven for. Gautama is very precise when he defines perfect persons as those who carry right thoughts in their minds. His understanding of right thoughts, too, is very precise. They are thoughts of selflessness and benevolence. A person with such thoughts is an *arahat*, an enlightened person, someone who has entered *nirvana*. On the contrary, one who is engrossed in negative thoughts of covetousness and ill-will remains imprisoned in *samsara*.

In order to continually cherish thoughts of selflessness and benevolence a relentless effort is required. One may ask why such an effort is necessary in acquiring such a simple thing as thoughts of selflessness and benevolence. The answer is to be found in the earlier discussion on the Second Noble Truth. Through the doctrines of Dependent Origination and that of mind-body, we have seen that humans have no control over their own thoughts. Senses control human thoughts, generating feelings of covetousness and enmity. Therefore, if persons are to exercise control over their own minds and fill them with thoughts of benevolence, they must wage a relentless war with themselves. To win that war, Gautama says, a person must make continual effort.

For Gautama, the development of good thoughts is an art. Several sermons preached by him explain that art. In one sermon of the *Anguttara Nikaya* he shows that, if the effort is to bear fruit it should be pursued methodically and step by step (AN, II, 15, Sutta 13f.). He mentions four specific steps:

1. Individuals must first try to *prevent* unwholesome thoughts from entering the mind. For that they should stop the senses from flirting with sense objects.

2. If, however, the effort to prevent unwholesome thoughts has not been totally successful, they should make an effort to *abandon* those that have entered the mind.

3. But the individuals' target is not achieved purely by abandoning bad thoughts. They must *develop* wholesome thoughts.

4. The fourth step is the effort to *retain* as permanently as possible the wholesome thoughts so developed.

These four steps illustrate the systematic nature of Gautama's plan for training the mind.

A second sermon in which several equally practical counsels are given is the twentieth discourse of the *Majjhima Nikaya*, which outlines a series of steps to be followed in the struggle against evil thoughts (MN, Sutta 20). Briefly paraphrased, the three most important counsels are:

1. If a particular object causes evil desires, try to bring before your mind another object that will remove those bad thoughts and generate good ones.

2. If the evil thoughts still persist, try to visualize the painful consequences that will follow if these covetous and inimical plans are executed.

3. Finally, if that too is of no help, change the environment.

There is no need to say how practical and how psychologically apt these directives are.[7] These instructions of Gautama on the art of developing wholesome thoughts clearly illustrate what Right Effort is and how it leads a person to liberation. This doctrine of Right Effort could be of particular interest to the modern educator or the religion teacher whose main interest is the development of character.

Today everyone admits that the primary aim of religious instruction is not the imparting of information on dogmas and doctrines, but the formation of character. But few teachers are able to achieve that aim successfully, because they are unable to state specifically what constitutes good character. In finding the right answer, Gautama's view here is particularly significant. *For him, persons of good character are those who always have good thoughts in their minds, and good thoughts are thoughts of selflessness and benevolence.*

Accordingly, to the religious educator, building of character becomes the same thing as transforming thought. To the extent that teachers induce students to develop thoughts of selflessness and friendliness, they build up their personalities.

In the next two chapters, we shall see two areas in which Right Effort is particularly applicable: the development of mindfulness, and the practice of meditation.

Chapter Thirteen

Right Mindfulness

Most Buddhist manuals translate *samma sati*, the seventh step of the Eightfold Path, as Right Mindfulness. But a more intelligible rendering for the modern reader would be Right Attentiveness, for without any doubt attentiveness to reality in its diverse levels is what Gautama understood by *sati*.

Whether we term it "attentiveness" or "mindfulness," the truth implied thereby is something that is very close to the heart of Gautama. The two steps of the Eightfold Path that one could underline as particularly characteristic of his doctrine of liberation are Right Understanding, the first, and Right Attentiveness, the seventh. Any individual intent on overcoming the sorrows of life has to understand reality first, and then all the while be attentive to its implications in day-to-day life.

Attentiveness to reality was the very aim of meditation itself (the subject of the next chapter). Meditation was related to attentiveness as the boat to the harbor. Meditation was the way. Attentiveness to reality was the goal.

Sermon on Mindfulness

The principal exposition of Gautama on the subject is called the *Satipatthana Sutta*, "The Sermon on the Arousing of Mindfulness" (MN, Sutta 10; DN, Sutta 22). This is the central text upon which a student must depend in order to discover its meaning.

"Mindfulness" (*sati*) was for Gautama one of the most important steps to be taken in the effort to achieve liberation. The opening words of his instruction on mindfulness make that clear: "This is the only way, monks, to purify beings, surmount sorrow and lamentation, destroy pain and grief, reach the right paths, and realize *nirvana*; it is the way... of mindfulness."

In this sermon Gautama speaks of attentiveness to reality in three different forms or levels:

1. attentiveness to whatever is being done at a particular moment,
2. attentiveness to the reality of life and particularly to the transience of life,
3. attentiveness to inner impulses.

Attentiveness to What Is Being Done

Persons who have achieved mastery over themselves, or who are on the way to self-mastery (liberation), are attentive to every action they do at any given moment. Average persons are not capable of such attentiveness, because their senses and mind lack the coordination required for it. As an illustration, let us consider a father returning from work. His 6-year-old child rushes to tell him a story about something that happened at school. The father turns to the child and apparently listens to him, but his *mind* is dwelling on something that his boss has said to him at the office. His *ears* are with the son, but not his mind. Or in the case of a young woman who is reading a book, her eyes may be on the page of the book but her mind is on a dress that she would like to buy.

According to Buddhism, liberated persons are different. For them, at any given moment, the work in front of them is of total importance. They attend to it with all the power of mind and heart. They are not preoccupied with anything else. They are not distracted.

To develop this form of attentiveness or alertness, Gautama recommends an exercise that is very effective and easy to practice. Each day persons should spend a little time in focusing their attention on different movements of the body or on different actions they are performing. During this exercise, they verbalize their actions in their mind. If they are walking, they say to themselves, "I am now walking." If they are sitting or lying down, they say, "I am now sitting," "I am now lying down."

Such an attention-training exercise frequently practiced can be helpful to those who wish to be more attentive to what they are doing, whether it be reading a book, listening to a child, or talking to a friend.

Another exercise recommended by Gautama is called the "exercise of in-and-out-breathing." This, in fact, is easier and even more effective and will be explained in the chapter on meditation (chap. 14), because it also leads to what is called "the calming of the mind."

In modern society individuals may use the above exercises, or others that they may know of, but they cannot escape the fact that attentiveness to whatever they are doing at any given moment is a proficiency for which they have to strive earnestly.

Attentiveness to the Realities of Life

The second aspect of mindfulness differs little from the term "insight" or the term "Right Understanding." Truly mature persons will always be aware of the realities of life that lie beneath external appearances. For them emotional life is transient, painful, and non-autonomous (*anicca, dukkha, anatta*). They will see that pleasure, possessions, and positions lack value as ultimate ends.

To achieve mindfulness in this deepest sense, Gautama has recommended in the Sermon on Mindfulness an exercise that is very effective. It is called the cemetery meditation. Persons should periodically think of their death and what will happen to their body after death. "Again, if he sees a dead body... he contemplates his own body thus: Verily this body of mine is of the same nature; it will become like that—I will not escape from it."

Attentiveness to Inner Impulses

The third facet of mindfulness, and the one that, we have to say, is most representative of its specific sense, is attentiveness to the inner impulses that underlie a person's day-to-day actions. In the Sermon on Mindfulness (*Satipatthana Sutta*) this is referred to as "contemplation of the mind." According to Gautama, persons intent on experiencing liberation in the full sense of the word should learn the art of scrutinizing the state of their minds at the very moment they are saying or doing something.

The justification behind that directive is self-evident. Immature human beings do not act rationally. More often than not, they are moved by emotions like a puppet by its strings. What is still worse, even when they act under the impulse of emotions, they do not want to own up to that fact. Often, they want to camouflage it by resorting to rationalizations or false reasons. A husband, for example, may criticize his wife for bad cooking, when the real basis for his criticism is his suspicion that she is friendly with another man. Had he scrutinized his mind at that moment, he would have known that his problem was not one of tasteless food but of jealousy.

Persons who are interested in acting rationally and objectively should constantly search their minds for the real motives behind their actions, and recognize them for what they are. If they are bad, they should recognize them as such. Feelings of hatred, pride, shyness, lust, despair, and jealousy are bad. If their feelings are good-feelings of friendliness, gentleness, confidence, honesty— they should also recognize them for what they are. To quote Gautama's own words in the Sermon on Mindfulness:

> And how does a monk practice mind-contemplation? Herein the monk knows the mind

115

with lust as being with lust, the mind without lust as being without lust, the mind with hate as being with hate, the mind without hate as being without hate, the mind with delusion as being with delusion, the mind without delusion as being without delusion.

This exercise of mindfulness has a distant resemblance to the "examination of conscience" practiced by some Christians and Jews, and particularly monks and nuns before they retire at night. But the two should not be confused with each other, for they are not identical. In Buddhism, the examination of conscience takes place at the very moment that the individual is performing an action and not at a later hour or on Yom Kippur. Further, its purpose is not just to assess the rightness or wrongness of an action. It does something more. It tries to analyze the inner structure of the mind at the moment an action is being performed. Such mind-analysis has in itself a great curative power. It immediately and automatically drives away harmful emotions. Emotions dissolve under scrutiny, as ice under sunlight.

When mindfulness in that very specific form is taken into account, it is not difficult to understand why Gautama considered it so fundamental to a liberated life, which in reality is a life of self-mastery.

These are the three aspects of attentiveness to reality that delineate the importance attached to it by Gautama. In fact, it was mindfulness that he recommended to his disciples from his deathbed. His last words were: "Emotional life is transient. Strive ahead with attentiveness" (*Vayadhamma samkhara appamadena sampadeta*).[8]

Attentiveness was also insisted upon by Jesus. The parable of the five wise virgins and the five foolish virgins illustrates the importance he attached to it. In that parable, the five wise virgins kept vigil for the return of the bridegroom, but the five foolish did not; the bridegroom returned unexpectedly and the five wise ones entered with him into the celebration, whereas the five foolish ones were excluded. "So, stay awake, because you do not know the day or the hour" (Matt. 25:1-13).

Rabbi Jochanan ben Zakki, a younger contemporary of Jesus, related a strikingly similar parable:

> This may be compared to a king who summoned his servants to a banquet without appointing a time. The wise ones adorned themselves and sat at the door of the palace, for they said, "is anything lacking in a royal palace?" [A summons may come at any time.] The fools went about their work saying, "can there be a banquet without preparation?" Suddenly the king desired the presence of his servants: the wise ones entered adorned, while the fools entered soiled. The king rejoiced at the wise but was angry with the fools. "Those who adorned themselves for the banquet," he ordered, "let them sit, eat, and drink. But those who did not adorn themselves for the banquet, let them stand and watch."[9]

In Judaism and Christianity, the idea of mindfulness is expressed constantly through the image of a person expecting the return of the master, and buried within this image is an insistence upon the sense of responsibility that should accompany the most ordinary daily activities of an individual. It is such a person who is said in Christianity and Judaism to be "saved."

The three dimensions of attentiveness to reality illustrate the relevance that Gautama's teaching has for all time. There is no need to emphasize that the practice of Right Mindfulness can substantially enrich the life of any individual today, even as in Gautama's time.

Chapter Fourteen

Right Concentration

The Pali word rendered here as "concentration" is *samadhi*, and "concentration" is the term commonly used in Buddhist manuals. But it is doubtful that "concentration" conveys to a Westerner the full reality implied by the term. To a Westerner "concentration" does not have any particularly religious import.

Etymologically, *sam-a-dha* means "keeping oneself (or one's thoughts) in the right place." It thus means to be "self-collected." Probably a term such as "self-collectedness" or "recollected-ness" would better convey to a Westerner the idea behind *samadhi*.

Persons who are self-collected are not distracted. Their thoughts are not dispersed. They are not preoccupied with useless or unimportant details. Their thoughts are always focused on the right goals. They are not disturbed by the vicissitudes of life. In the sense explained in the previous chapter, they are also always "mindful." Consequently, they are in a constant state of peace and mental rest. If not construed to mean a behavior that is negative or purely passive, then "peacefulness," "mental harmony," or "mental rest" would be equally good renderings of the term *samadhi*.

However, the best way to understand *samadhi* is to study the means recommended by Gautama to achieve it. The means is meditation, *bhavana. Bhavana* is the way to *samadhi* in all Indian religions, but in Buddhism both *samadhi* and *bhavana* have certain nuances of their own.

Meditation is an aspect of Buddhism in which a growing interest can be noticed among non-Buddhists, particularly of the West. Nonetheless, there are some widespread misconceptions about it.

Many Westerners, for instance, think that Buddhism is purely and simply a form of meditation. That is not true. In examining the Eightfold Path, we see that meditation comes under only one of its eight elements. That is an important fact to keep in mind, for meditation cannot be rightly appreciated if its significance is exaggerated.

Meditation is an exercise that should not appear foreign to Christians and Jews. It would be wrong for them to think that meditation is totally different from prayer. Meditation may differ from petitionary prayer, but petitionary prayer is not the only type of prayer known to Jews and Christians. Meditative prayer, silent prayer, contemplation, and mental prayer as practiced by Christians and Jews come under the same category of religious experience as that of Buddhist meditation. This is not to say that there are no differences at all, but the differences have to do much less with the goal than with the way to the goal. Jews and Christians believe in a personal God, and so their prayers are conversational in character. Oriental meditations are more reflective and non-conversational. Despite such differences, the aim of both prayer and meditation is to help persons face their day-to-day problems realistically and calmly.

Whatever the type of meditation studied—be it Hindu, Buddhist, Muslim, Jewish, or Christian—its reality is most easily grasped by seeing it as performing two functions. Buddhist meditation defines the precise nature of these two functions:

1. calming of the mind (through *samatha bhavana* or "tranquility" meditation),

2. widening the mind's vision of the reality of life (through *vipassana bhavana* or "insight" meditation).

Calming the Mind

A basic function of meditation is to establish calmness in the mind that is ordinarily in a very perturbed state. All adults are in need of such a state of calm and, if meditation is to be meaningful, those who engage in it must first recognize the perturbed state of their own minds. They should be aware that they are victims of anxiety, fear, disappointment, frustration, and a sense of abandonment. Material comforts cannot dispel this perturbed state of mind.

A few who find this turbulent state too burdensome escape from it in suicide. Many seek relief through drugs or alcohol, which produce only a temporary release from tension. More popular techniques providing temporary relaxation are smoking, chewing gum, chewing betel, or drinking tea or coffee.

Meditation is a more helpful technique because it diverts the mind from its preoccupations with longer-lasting effect. Meditation does so by making the mind concentrate on a new fictitious object of attention. If the new object is to draw the attention of the mind successfully, it must be both proximate (a movement of the body or an object that is within the range of visibility) and non-burdensome. This strategy for diverting attention illustrates why oriental religious meditation is also called "concentration." The fictitious object of concentration newly presented to the senses divests the mind of its tiredness and nervous tension.

When such exercises are repeated, the attention of the mind is more permanently diverted from its earlier concerns, for they then begin to lose their binding power. Tensions gradually disappear, and the mind thereby becomes relaxed enough to look back on its earlier preoccupations and to examine them without a sense of oppression. That, in a general way, is the inner working of meditation that produces calm (*samatha bhavana*). Its inner working is illustrated in **Figure 7** (see next page).

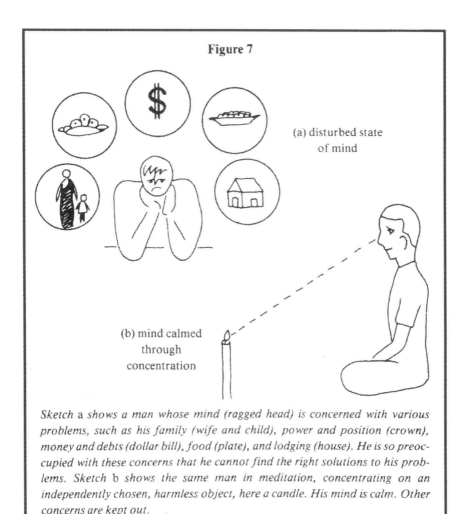

Figure 7

(a) disturbed state
of mind

(b) mind calmed
through
concentration

Sketch a shows a man whose mind (ragged head) is concerned with various problems, such as his family (wife and child), power and position (crown), money and debts (dollar bill), food (plate), and lodging (house). He is so preoccupied with these concerns that he cannot find the right solutions to his problems. Sketch b shows the same man in meditation, concentrating on an independently chosen, harmless object, here a candle. His mind is calm. Other concerns are kept out.

Objects chosen for concentration vary and many have been used in the Buddhist tradition. The one cherished most by Gautama in his personal meditation, and the one most insistently recommended for use by his disciples, is known as "in-and-out-breathing" (*anapana sati*). It is an easy exercise to practice and it can be practiced anywhere—at home, in a park, in a bus, in a train. All that is required is to focus attention on one's breath, as it is inhaled and as it is exhaled. The duration of the inhalation and exhalation does not

121

matter. All that is necessary is to concentrate one's attention on the breathing action without permitting the mind to be diverted by other objects. Because breathing is an action within one's body, and is the only bodily action that can be physically controlled (unlike the heartbeat or the circulation of blood), its attention-retaining power is very great, which explains its value as an effective object of concentration. (Such concentration on breathing is not the same as breathing exercises adopted in physiotherapy, the purpose of which is to improve the functioning of the lungs.)

Inasmuch as this meditation of "in-and-out-breathing" has characterized the Buddhist tradition, it may be of value to quote Gautama's explanation:

> And how does a monk live practicing body-contemplation...? Herein a monk having gone to the forest, to the foot of a tree, or to a lonely place, sits down cross-legged keeping the body erect and his mindfulness alert, mindful he breathes in, mindful he breathes out. When breathing in a long breath, he knows: "I breathe in a long breath." When breathing in a short breath, he knows, "I breathe in a short breath." When breathing out a long breath, he knows, "I breathe out a long breath." When breathing out a short breath, he knows, "I breathe out a short breath."
>
> "Conscious of the entire process, I will breathe in." Thus, he trains himself. "Conscious of the entire process, I will breathe out." Thus, he trains himself [Mahasatipatthana Sutta (DN, Sutta 22)].

Though breathing is the most recommended object of concentration in Buddhism, a number of other objects also are mentioned: a flame, a colored disc, the tip of one's nose. The recitation of beads (a practice found among Catholics, Buddhists, Hindus, and Muslims) can have the same effect as concentration on breathing. The same is true

122

of the mantra recitation practiced by those following Transcendental Meditation (a form of Indian meditation popular in the West in the 1970s). In these techniques, the object of concentration is the physical act of recitation; the movements of the fingers and lips are of additional help. Such effortless physical movements retain and absorb the attention of the mind, diverting it from other mind-preoccupying objects. As a result, the mind is released from fatigue and tension.

Widening the Vision of Reality

Though the calming of the mind is an important effect of meditation, it is neither the only effect nor the most important. For the mind to be strengthened to face daily problems squarely, it must be enriched by an objective view of reality. This means that, without escaping from the objects that preoccupy it, the mind must now return to them and view them from a new and more realistic perspective. Gautama views life and reality as *anicca, dukkha anatta*—"transient, painful, and illusory." According to Gautama, such a view of life can be achieved only by what is called "insight" (*vi-passana*).

Realism. One topic of meditation leading to the reality of life is the cemetery meditation. Frequent concentration on death and the bodily corruption that follows it leads one to a mature understanding of life. Adults see life as it is—as transient, painful, illusory. Adults accept themselves as they are. They accept illness, old age, and death as parts of life. They do not grumble or fret about them. When some misfortune happens, they never say, "Such things do not happen to others: they happen only to me." They accept pain, suffering, and disappointment as a part of every life, even that of the apparently most successful persons.

Gautama's "insight" approach to reality, in comparison with the attitude of the theistic religions, may appear somewhat ruthless. In facing the problems of life, such as failure, sickness, and death, an

123

adherent of the theistic religions is accustomed to being told, "Do not be anxious about your problems. God is there. God will protect you." Through the insight doctrine of *anicca-dukkha-anatta*, Gautama says, "Life is exactly like that. It is transient, painful, illusory. Accept it as it is. Do not be a baby. Face up to it as an adult should. Train and strengthen yourself, through 'insight meditation' to accept the reality of life."

Benevolence. Along with the acceptance of oneself as one is, insight meditation leads one to accept others as those to whom one is related and toward whom one must extend friendship. In order to awaken oneself to this spirit of benevolence toward all, Gautama recommended the practice of another characteristic form of meditation called "friendship meditation," *maitri bhavana*. Gautama viewed this meditation as one endowed with extraordinary maturity-building value.

Its practice is as follows. At any suitable moment, meditators send out thoughts of good will toward different individuals, beginning with those whom they love—parents, siblings, spouse, children. They then include those with whom their relationship is of a general nature, such as fellow students, co-workers, pupils, and servants. Finally, they incorporate those whom they dislike and who are inimical to them. In each instance, they identify them by name, individually, in their minds and express this or a similar phrase of well-wishing: May (name) be happy, may he (she) be in good health, may she (he) prosper.

Such wishes of benevolence, according to Gautama, strengthen the mind and enlarge the heart of the well-wisher. Such a spirit of loving kindness was a basic quality that Gautama tried to inculcate in his disciples. The insistence with which he did so is evident from his advice:

> Monks, if a person were to harbor ill-will even
> when wild bandits with a double-handed saw were
> to dismember him, he is not a follower of my
> teaching. Thus, monks, should you train

yourselves. "Unsullied shall our minds remain, neither shall an ill-word escape our lips, but kindly and compassionate, we will ever abide with loving hearts and not harbor hate. We will radiate loving kindness even to them [bandits] and then we will radiate the whole world with thoughts of infinite friendliness, without hate, without ill-will." This is how you must train yourselves, monks [MN, I, 130, Sutta 21].

Gautama believed that by the power of loving-kindness a person could tame enemies and even wild animals. Stories in the scriptures show that Gautama demonstrated this in action. The winning of Roja the Malla, an adversary of Gautama's, the taming of the "demon" Alkavaka, the conversion of the ruthless robber Angulimala, and the controlling of the drunken elephant Nalagiri are examples of such actions. Gautama's motto in this regard is clearly expressed in the following verse of the *Dhammapada*:

> Hatred never by hatred,
> Is appeased in this world,
> By love alone is it appeased,
> This is an ancient principle
> [chap. 1, 5].

Three other related qualities to be developed by means of meditation are compassion (*karuna*), gentleness (*mudita*), and equanimity (*upekkha*).

Such, in brief, is the concept of meditation in Buddhism. In its simplest definition, meditation is a practice of mental concentration that brings the two elements of *calm* and *realism* to a perturbed, blind mind. Thus, an individual who meditates is able to face squarely all life situations with a full grasp of reality and with a spirit of benevolence.

The best summarization of the Buddhist system of meditation is the advice given by Gautama to his son Venerable Rahula. The advice enumerates the principal types of meditation that are specifically Buddhist in character:

> Develop the meditation on loving kindness (*metta*), Rahula, for by this ill-will is banished.
> Develop the meditation on compassion (*karuna*), Rahula, for by this cruelty is banished.
> Develop the meditation on gentleness (*mudita*), Rahula, for by this hard-heartedness is banished.
> Develop the meditation on equanimity (*upekkha*), Rahula, for by this anxiety is banished.
> Develop the meditation on the corruptibility of the body (*asubha*), Rahula, for by this lust is banished.
> Develop the meditation on the concept of impermanence (*anicca*), Rahula, for by this the pride of self (*asmi-mana*) is banished.
> Develop the concentration of mindfulness by in- and-out breathing (*anapana sati*), Rahula, for this, if frequently practiced, bears much fruit and is of great advantage [MN, I, 424, Sutta 62].

The exposition on Right Meditation concludes our study of the Eightfold Path. The Eightfold Path, the fourth of the Noble Truths, is also the most basic of the four truths. The other three are meant only to show why this path is the right path, and why, though very simple, it is sufficient by itself. If we now sum up in brief the thought behind each of the Four Noble Truths, it would be as follows:

First Noble Truth. A sorrowfulness of a very deep type is the common lot of humankind. There is nobody who does not experience it or suffer from it. (The purpose of a religion is to liberate humanity from it.)

Second Noble Truth. The cause of this innate sorrow is within humanity itself. It is disoriented desire arising from an emotional and unenlightened view of life.

Third Noble Truth. However innate or universal this sorrow be, humans can overcome it. It is within the power of every human being to achieve a life of peace and inner joy.

Fourth Noble Truth. A very appropriate path to it is the Eightfold Path, of which the key element is a right understanding of life. An enlightened view of life is by itself a medicine endowed with a sure curative power. (The best religion, therefore, is that of the Eightfold Path.)

HUMAN LIBERATION: THE INNER AFFINITY AMONG THE VIEWS OF GAUTAMA, YESHUA, AND JUDAISM

Chapter Fifteen

The Challenge of the Four Noble Truths

Thus far we have looked in some detail at the teaching contained in the Four Noble Truths. We have taken the four truths one by one, and some of them even part by part. Inasmuch as the Four Noble Truths are generally assumed to be a summarization of Gautama's entire philosophy, we might now conclude that we have a comprehensive idea of what Buddhism is.

But here we must be careful and not be in too much of a hurry. It is true that each of the Four Noble Truths taken individually teaches many great lessons. But there is more to the Four Noble Truths than is contained in each of them. The main lesson or the real challenge of the Four Noble Truths does not become evident when they are considered individually. And no one could be said to have grasped Gautama's philosophy fully if the main lesson of the Four Noble Truths is not grasped.

For Gautama, the Four Noble Truths were not four distinct metaphysical assertions. For him they were four parts of just one proposition. They were meant to be taken as a whole, because together they formed one logical syllogism. Through them he is arguing a point, and a very challenging point at that. The first three truths are the premises of the syllogism. The fourth is the conclusion flowing from them.

Therefore, if we are not to miss the real force and punch of this great sermon, we must take the four truths together as a whole, as integral parts of one single argument. If we are to understand the sermon in its full vigor, we must not lose sight of Gautama's motive behind it. *Why* he preached the Four Noble Truths has in that sense as great a lesson to teach as *what* he preached in them.

What then, in brief, is the argument of the Four Noble Truths? What is it all about? What does it assert? And what does it oppose? Purely and simply, the argument of the Four Noble Truths is about the meaning and function of religion. In it, Gautama is contesting the popularly upheld definitions of religion, and presenting in their place a new one of his own. The definitions of religion that were put forward in his day all seemed to him vague, inaccurate, impractical, and thus misleading. Against them he sets forth one that purports to be simple, precise, logical, and practical.

One could of course here ask the question why Gautama should spend time and energy defining such an elementary thing as religion. Is not the nature of religion obvious to everybody? The simple fact is that it is not. As a general rule, religion is regarded as something that everybody knows all about. And there is of course a justification for that attitude. In the case of the majority of us, religion is a natural ingredient of our lives. It is part of our family tradition or national heritage. Most of us have been born into the religion we profess. We are so used to it and take it so much for granted that we feel we could define it easily if we were asked to. We do not realize that there is probably nothing in the world more difficult to define than religion.

If we want to be convinced of that, we have only to turn to a few of our companions and ask a very simple question: In your opinion, what is religion? What is its primary function? We would be surprised to discover that ten individuals would probably answer it in ten different ways.

One would begin by referring to belief in God, or gods and goddesses. Another would start by speaking of churches and temples, festivals and pilgrimages. A third would speak of rites and rituals and of priests who officiate at them. A fourth would speak of monks and nuns. A fifth would speak of religion as a collective authority that safeguards moral values in society. For still another it would be a quasi-political force that ensures unity in a community or a nation. There would be many other explanations.

There is of course no doubt that these aspects of religion have their value, and so are to be respected. But the question is: Do any of them touch religion in its essence? Do they pinpoint what religion has first and foremost and at all costs to achieve? Do they touch the problems of disadvantaged human beings, and their cure? Do they bring out the liberational aspect of religion?

It is this same issue that was before Gautama's eyes when he decided to set out on his preaching mission. He saw, as nobody else in his day had done, that when it came to religion, human beings had lost their sense of priorities. They saw a number of things under the name of religion, but not what was central and basic to it. In religious matters, they were uncertain as to where the accent should be placed. And so, Gautama felt that his mission would be fruitless if he did not start by carefully defining religion in its essence. That is why he began with the statement known to us today as the Four Noble Truths.

The simple aim of the Four Noble Truths is to define religion with regard to its primary purpose. Religion as he saw it had to be an answer to a concrete human problem. It had to be a *medicine* to a definite human ailment. To put it more technically, it had to bring about a liberation. A religion that did not offer liberation was for him no religion at all. To liberate human beings was for him the primary function of religion.

With reference to himself, liberation was all that Gautama sought from religion; it was also only liberation that he wanted to bring to others through religion. This is very clear from the instruction he gave his very first group of missionaries as he sent them out to preach. He said: "I am *liberated*, monks, from all ties earthly and non-earthly. You are also *liberated* from all ties earthly and non-earthly. Go now and wander for the welfare and the happiness of the many" (VP/MV, chap. 1, 19).

But, of course, to explain religion to our contemporaries through liberation is to explain the unknown by the unknown. Liberation, taken in its religious sense, is a word that is as ambiguous as religion itself.

Religion as Liberation

The English word "liberation" comes from the Latin term *liberare*, which means "to free" or "to give freedom to." In the context in which the term was originally used, it referred to the releasing of slaves or prisoners. In the course of time, however, the word acquired a symbolic sense, and began to have a wider application. Release from any situation that, like corporeal slavery or imprisonment, was an obstacle to human happiness or human fulfillment was referred to as liberation. It is in that symbolic sense that the term is more commonly used today.

Liberation, however, is not a term that is reserved for religious usage. Wherever there exists an obstacle to human happiness, there is the possibility of a liberation. And so, liberation is a term that is widely used in contemporary secular society. In secular society, we speak of doctors who liberate the sick from their sicknesses. We speak of economic institutions that liberate the poor from their poverty. We speak of teachers who liberate children from their ignorance. In all these instances too, liberation is used in a symbolic sense. But the employment of the term is such that there is no room whatsoever for doubt as to what is meant.

Doubts arise only when it is applied to religion. In the case of religious liberation, nobody has a clear idea as to the state of "slavery" or "bondage" from which the "victim" is to be liberated. A Jew or a Christian might refer to it as "sin," "the devil," or "hell." But the meaning of these terms is so vague and so blurred in the minds of ordinary persons that many today tend to ask whether religious liberation is half as relevant in modern society as the other forms of liberation, such as the medical, economic, or the educational.

Jews and Christians who venture upon a comparison of Christianity and Judaism with Buddhism have to give serious thought to Gautama's thesis about the link between religion and liberation. Liberation is not, of course, a notion that is exclusive to Buddhism. It is common to Judaism and Christianity too, as to all religions. In all religions, the liberation theme plays a pivotal role. It is so central to any religion that around it all other doctrines rotate like a door on a hinge.

But unfortunately, that is so only in theory. In practice liberation is the notion that is mostly left unexplained and unexplored in religion classes. Worse still, religious doctrines are often taught as independent units with no reference to their connection with liberation. In classes on Christianity for example, it is not rare to find teachers who take great pains in explaining doctrinal tenets such as God, Trinity, incarnation, sacraments, or commandments. In Judaism it is much the same with lessons about Torah, kashrut, halakha, peoplehood, the land. They consider these as treatises by themselves. Nothing is done to show students the link that exists between one another, either of the teachings themselves or of the teachings with liberation. Thus, religion becomes in the eyes of the student simply a heap of disconnected doctrines.

The approach of such teachers is very similar to that of a teacher of mechanics who, in teaching students about an engine, dismantles an engine, heaps the parts together, and explains them one by one as each comes to hand. Even if they understood each part as a separate entity, students could not have grasped how each part combined with the others to make the vehicle move.

Any one part of an engine is understood only when it is seen in its role of making a vehicle *move*. In the same way, a religious doctrine is correctly understood only when it is seen in its role of helping persons to *liberate* themselves. No religious teaching, however impressively it may be formulated, has any value except as part of a system that effects the liberation of the human person.

Liberation as Personality Development

If the notion of liberation is thus relegated to an out-of-the-way corner, the reason for it is not hard to find. Many of us have no clear idea what religious liberation is all about because we are not sincerely convinced that we are internally ailing. If one is not aware of an ailment, one is not going to look for a cure. On the other hand, we could not be blamed for not having an idea of this inner human malady. It is not something we can see with our eyes.

With our eyes, we can see the *exterior physical personality* of an individual and observe any exterior tragedy that affects him or her. But we need something more than even x-ray eyes to see the *inner mental personality* of the same individual. But Gautama, who had extensively developed his power of "insight," was able to discern clearly what earthly beings, such as we, could at best only suspect—namely, that persons who looked physically and exteriorly perfect could, deep within themselves, be sick and deformed.

In his view, human beings were victims of something more than the commonly spoken of tragedies of ignorance, illness, or poverty. Such exterior deficiencies could be remedied by teachers, doctors, and economists. But there was an illness of the spirit, an ignorance of the spirit, and a poverty of the spirit much more radical and much more damaging. Jealousy, anger, lust, greed, hatred, laziness were the internal symptoms of this depraved condition of the spirit. These were a greater obstacle to human happiness than was any physical sickness, lack of schooling, or shortage of money. As a matter of fact, most people who were quite healthy physically, well qualified academically, and very comfortable materially were unhappy.

It is this sad state of the human condition and the manner of overcoming it that Gautama described in the Four Noble Truths. In the first, he defines the sickly state of a person's mind, or of the malfunctioning state of someone's "humanhood." This state is characterized by mental anguish, *dukkha*. In the second, he describes the reason behind this malfunctioning, which is self-centeredness in behavior due to emotionalism in making judgments. The third shows the fullness of life that one could enjoy when this mental weakness is overcome. The fourth describes the techniques to be followed on the path to liberation from this human tragedy.

An understanding of the Four Noble Truths in this deep sense brings out very clearly one point in Gautama's thought pattern. For him liberation is a personality transformation. Liberation conducts individuals from their underdeveloped state of personhood to a fully developed state—and the sphere in which the transformation takes place is none other than the mind.

It would have made things much simpler had we been able to define Gautama's religious liberation directly in terms of personality development. But unfortunately, the word "personality" has been so much debased in current usage that such a definition could lead to gross misunderstandings. Personality at times is used in reference to the external appearance of an individual—an appearance that can be enhanced by the use of cosmetics or well-tailored clothes. At times, it is used in reference to an individual's career-advancement abilities—abilities that can lead to fame, popularity, money, position. With the possibility of such a variety of interpretations, to use the expression "personality development" for the type of deep mental transformation that Gautama envisaged could be hazardous.

But if misunderstandings could be avoided, and personality could be taken as an equivalent for an individual's inner adulthood, then it would be correct to say that liberation for Gautama was basically personality development, for the development of the *human person* was his primary concern. Expressed differently, his aim was to transform the human child into the human adult.

The techniques that he advocated for such a personality development he enumerated in his Eightfold Path. The eight steps of that path are by themselves a proof that what he understood by liberation was clearly a matter of personality transformation. Noble behavior in day-to-day life through Right Thoughts, Right Speech, Right Action, Right Livelihood was fundamental, because it is that which transforms an individual into an adult. The most important of course was Right Understanding, the step named first in the path. The Right Understanding that was desired was of one's "self" and of life as such. It was Right Understanding that one had to practice every moment through Right Mindfulness. That was what one had to acquire through Right Meditation. All these elements show that according to Gautama the liberation most needed by humanity was that of passing over from childishness to adulthood.

What he excluded from the Eightfold Path is as much indicative of his notion of liberation as what he included in it. Rites and rituals, penances and asceticism, worship of gods and goddesses are not aspects that were left out of the path due to some inadvertence. The omission was intentional, and he wanted to show positively that they were not strictly necessary. They contributed nothing positive to personality development. What was fundamental for an effective personality uplift was the awakening of the sleeping mind of men and women, or the broadening of their vision to reality in its fullness.

The main function of religion as Gautama saw it was education. Religion was for him like a school of the highest level, such as a university. The subject that this particular type of university specialized in was not botany, physics, or chemistry, but adulthood—growth into human excellence. Missionaries were preeminently teachers of adulthood. They were of course not teachers of the traditional schoolteacher type, who primarily are informers about arts and sciences. Missionaries are educators, and a special type of educator, because they are awakeners. They awakened others from a kind of sleeping sickness. In a way, their role was close to that of doctors because the awakening led to a healing of the mind. Religious ministry thus for Gautama was a ministry of education and of healing.

It is this thought of Gautama's concealed behind the doctrine of the Four Noble Truths that has to be grasped well by a student who wishes to comprehend Gautama's message in depth and in its totality. It is this Buddhist view of religion and liberation that becomes a real challenge to religious women and men of all times.

Quite naturally it is this argumentation of Gautama's that should form the framework in a meaningful comparison of Judaism and Christianity with Buddhism. Are Judaism and Christianity also religions in the sense that Gautama understood it? Was personality transformation as fundamental to Jesus and the Rabbis as it was to Gautama? These are the basic questions that Christian and Jewish students will have to answer. But even before they begin answering them, there is a major question that is bound to intervene. That is the question of belief in God. Can belief in God, which is so central to Judaism and Christianity, be accommodated within a view of religious liberation that is purely a personality uplift?

These are some of the questions that will be discussed in the following pages as a help to the Christian and the Jew who wish to engage in a comparison of the three religions. Because the problem of belief in God is the main issue in any comparison of Buddhism with Judaism and Christianity, it is here discussed first, in the next two chapters.

Liberation Theology

Just before moving on, however, it would be well to comment here briefly on the great movement within Christianity since the mid—1960s—namely, liberation theology. What it entails is the systematic elaboration of the social implications of the gospel of Jesus. It is argued that the good news of how to live a full human life must be proclaimed to the whole of humanity, not so much quantitatively as qualitatively. That is, the social patterns by which human beings relate to each other are in fact essential elements of our humanity. It is not sufficient to attempt to liberate individual persons one by one, simply because in very many instances it will not work. Societal patterns have to be changed so that they foster rather than hinder the living of a fully liberated human life.

Thus, Christian liberation theology (which might more aptly be called "political theology," in line with Johannes Metz) argues that all persons are responsible to work for humanizing social structures as prerequisite conditions for a fully liberated human life. As mere conditions, these humanizing structures of course will not automatically lead to a fully liberated human life; for that, the personal liberation dimension of Jesus' gospel must also be realized. It has been an indispensable contribution by the West, whether Judeo-Christian or secular, to discern the absolute necessity of changing social structures if humanity is to be liberated. But even after such social structural change has been accomplished, other fundamental problems of human liberation remain. It is these that most of this book has focused on, assuming at the same time that social structural change must also be brought about.

It should also be noted that the same commitment to structural social change has characterized much of post—emancipation Judaism in the West—that is, in the nineteenth and twentieth centuries. The intellectual and activist involvement of countless thousands of individual Jews and a myriad of Jewish organizations to bring about wide and deep changes in social structures bears witness to this Jewish parallel to Christian socialism, the social gospel, and liberation theology.

Chapter Sixteen

Belief in God according to Gautama, Yeshua, and Judaism

The study so far should have made one central point indubitably clear: God is not part of Gautama's picture of human liberation. This is the most important factor of Buddhism that Jews and Christians have to seriously grapple with in their effort to compare Judaism and Christianity with Buddhism. If they are, however, to make any headway, they should begin by looking for the answer to two other important questions: Why was Gautama silent on the issue of God, and what was the attitude of Jesus and Judaism with regard to belief in God?

Gautama's Exclusion of God

Gautama's attitude toward the idea of God is very clear. Any concept of a supreme God, or worship of God in any ritualistic form, is for him totally unnecessary for liberation. Gautama's Eightfold Path, unlike its Judeo-Christian parallel, the Ten Commandments, contains no mention whatsoever of the worship of God. In a country such as India, where religion essentially consists of different paths to God or gods, the very exclusion of the idea makes Buddhism remarkably original.

With regard to this stand one important fact should be kept in mind. Although the concept of God was excluded from his path to liberation, Gautama never argued against it. He has at times shown the folly of blindly adhering to ritualistic practices. But hardly anywhere in his sermons can we find a direct attack on the concept of God. This is a valuable point to remember in assessing the Buddhist stand in regard to God.

If Gautama was not an antitheist at heart, what could have led him to violate all religious tradition and to omit from his religious philosophy a basic tenet of earlier religious systems? There seems to be no reason other than that the worship of God had by that time so greatly deteriorated that it distorted what Gautama considered to be the basic element in any religion—namely, liberation. As Jamshed K. Fazdar says in analyzing the state of Hinduism in Gautama's day:

> Religious inquiry was being choked by atrophied traditions which increasingly forced the blind acceptance of the Vedas as infallible dogma. The correct performance of ritual and ceremonies became all important, and was a constant source of contention and strife between different religious teachers, each claiming truth for his theory or practice, and frequently embroiling the civil and political authorities of his region in military action against those in "error."...
>
> To the Buddha, Hindu religion, which by then had become steeped in self-interest, class-prestige, and ecclesiastical niceties, seemed completely hollow [Fazdar, vi-vii].

According to Gautama, exponents of diverse forms of the worship of God tragically failed to focus attention on the liberation most urgently needed by humankind.

Gautama's stand in regard to God is very clear in a discussion that took place between Gautama and a monk named Malunkyaputta (*Majjhima Nikaya*, Sutta 63). The monk asks Gautama why he did not care to give a specific reply to questions such as: Is the world eternal, or is it not? Is it finite, or is it not? Is life in the body, or in the soul? Do beings continue after death, or do they not?

Gautama explained that if he did not speak of them, it was because they did not come within the ambit of his primary preoccupation. His concern was limited to a more urgent need for humanity. To explain his position, he told a very forceful story. Imagine that a man is going through a jungle. Halfway through he is shot by a poisoned arrow. If the poisoned arrow remains in his body, he will die. The injured person says: "I will not pull out this arrow until I know who shot it, whether he is tall or short, fat or lean, young or old, of a high caste or a low caste." I tell you, Malunkyaputta, says Gautama, that man will die before he knows the right answers.

For Gautama, the problem of internal human suffering was too concrete and too urgent to permit him to luxuriate on purely speculative questions not immediately relevant to the problem at hand. Speculative discussions on the nature of God, the origin of the world, or the nature of the soul are of no direct relevance to the basic issue. Gautama viewed human suffering, and the liberation from it, exactly as modern psychologists would look at mental patients in their clinics. They are concerned only with the sick state of the patients' minds, not with their religious theories.

That story is very revealing. Its objection to belief in God is radical and novel; it is doubtful whether any other opponent to the worship of God has approached it from the same perspective and with equal force. Gautama's question is not about whether God exists or not, but whether belief in God has any relevance to the immediate problems of humanity. In that sense, he cannot really be called an agnostic. It is true that like the agnostic he ignores the fact of God's existence. Nevertheless, his attitude toward God differs from that of the ordinary agnostic. The agnostic adopts an attitude of indifference, but Gautama is neither indifferent nor unconcerned. He is very concerned, but the object of his concern is humanity and its liberation, not God. Had he seen any recognizable link between human liberation and the concept of God, Gautama would have been the first to include the worship of God in his system of liberation.

141

There is thus a conspicuous difference between Gautama's objections to belief in God and those of the traditional atheist and agnostic. His argument against God is not leveled against religion. On the contrary, it is in the very name of religion, and as an attempt to save religion, that he omits the concept of God. Differently expressed, Gautama tells the believer in God: let us avoid the confusing and controversial concept of God, of divinity, and let us immediately work toward the divinization of humanity.

The Judeo-Christian Stance on Belief in God

What is the Christian and Jewish response to such a proposition? Before formulating an answer, we should look into the attitude that Jesus and the Judaism of his day had toward belief in God. It has many revealing factors.

For the sake of simplicity—and yet in the hope of avoiding oversimplification—and as a way of presenting the core of the Judeo-Christian teaching, in the rest of this book an attempt will be made to compare the teachings of Gautama with those of the prophets, Jesus, and the Rabbis. There was, in fact, a very great similarity among these three. The grounds for claiming this are that Jesus was a deeply committed, knowledgeable, devout Jew of his time—"I have come not to abolish the law, but to implement it" (Matt. 5:17). He stood in the Hebraic tradition of the prophets (he was often called a prophet by his contemporaries) and Rabbis, such as Hillel, before him (Jesus was addressed as "rabbi"). His notion of God as loving father was very much in line with that of the Pharisees of his day (the predecessors of the Rabbis and "founders" of Judaism); doubtless part of the reason for his at times intense debates with some Pharisees was the very closeness of his positions to many of theirs. (Much of the hostility exhibited toward the Pharisees in the Gospels stems not from Jesus but from the evangelists writing fifty to seventy years later in a church-synagogue polarized situation.)

The Jew Jesus espoused positions concerning God and liberation that fitted within the parameters of Judaism (this is not to be confused with what Christians later believed about Jesus the Christ), although he obviously took a direction within it peculiar to his own genius. Therefore, Jesus' and the Rabbis' views on the matter of liberation can be categorized together in order to compare them to the views of Gautama. To keep the Jewishness of Jesus at the forefront of the reader's consciousness, in the remaining pages Jesus will be referred to by the Hebrew form of his name, namely Yeshua, the one that, in fact, his contemporaries would have called him by.

To begin with, Yeshua frequently pointed out that there is a *wrong form* of worship of God, just as there is a right form. A typical example was his parable of a proud Pharisee and a despised tax collector (Luke 18:9-14).[10] Both were in the temple, and both were praying to God. "I thank you for my privileges," said the first. "God, be merciful to me a sinner," said the second. According to Yeshua, the prayer of the former was not a right type of worship of God, because the Pharisee had the wrong attitude toward himself. He was under an illusion regarding his self-importance. He was conceited, hypocritical, and pretentious. The latter's prayer, on the contrary, was a right type of worship of God, because the tax collector had a right understanding of himself. He was humble, self-accepting, and sincere.

Secondly, belief in God for the Hebrew prophets and Yeshua was not a matter of rite and ritual or of external formal worship, but a way of righteous living. We do not find them speaking of God with the aim of describing who God is. Whenever they spoke of belief in God, instead of spending their energy in describing the nature of God (as is at times done today in theological treatises) they spoke of the *qualities of the true believer*:

> What to me is the multitude of your sacrifices? says Yahweh;
> I have had enough of burnt offerings of rams and the fat of fed beasts....

143

Bring no more vain offerings; incense is an
abomination to me.
New moon and Sabbath and the calling of
assemblies—
I cannot endure festival and solemn
assembly....
Cease to do evil,
Learn to do good,
Seek justice,
Correct oppression,
Defend the orphan,
Plead for the widow [Isa. 1:11- 17].

I hate, I despise your feasts, and I take no delight in your solemn
assemblies.... But let justice roll like waters, and righteousness like
an ever-flowing stream [Amos 6:21, 24].

Yeshua's story of the good Samaritan has a similar message (Luke
10:29-37). In the Jewish view, the good Samaritan was not a true
believer in God. The two characters of the story who were
"professional" believers in God were the priest and the Levite.
When they met the man fallen on the road, they were probably on
their way to a ritual worship of God in the temple. But somehow
there was in this "unbelieving" Samaritan something of the right
form of worship of God that was not in the priest and the Levite.
The Samaritan stopped to help the traveler who had fallen victim to
brigands and cared for him to the extent of paying out of his own
pocket the injured man's medical expenses. It was him that Yeshua
upheld as a true worshiper of God. Judging from the story,
Yeshua's definition of the ideal worshiper of God in the given
instance is simply "the one who cares." For Yeshua, caring for a
needy person was a greater act of worship of God than was the
performance of even priestly functions.

Thirdly, Yeshua's attitude toward belief in God comes out very
clearly from the two parables just mentioned, as from all his other
assertions. The same attitude is found in the Hebrew prophets cited
earlier—and indeed, Judaism in general. None of them were ever

concerned about promoting a *conceptual knowledge* of God, or of creating in the minds of the people a clear mental picture of God's appearance. What they promoted exclusively was a *behavioral acknowledgment of God*.

In the first of Yeshua's stories, the caricatured Pharisee, being a religious scholar, may well have had a more articulated *concept* of God, and doubtless one that was much more learned than that of the religiously not so well-educated tax collector. But that did not help the Pharisee. In the case of the Samaritan of the second parable, it is doubtful that he had a *concept* of God acceptable to Yeshua's disciples and other fellow Jews. But he was a more authentic believer than were the priest and the Levite, who certainly had acceptable *concepts* or mental pictures of God. According to Yeshua's approach and that of the prophets, even atheists or agnostics, as long as they rightly fulfilled their duties in life, had the required qualification to be called believers in God.

True worshipers of God, according to them, are thus recognized not by the acts of formal worship that they perform but by the characteristics of their day-to-day behavior. The most central of course is loving care-concern-for those in need.

A fourth aspect is one that would bring Yeshua and the prophets still closer to Gautama in spirit. It is the attitude that could be called Yeshua's spirit of anti-ritualism—echoing loudly the tradition of the Hebrew prophets. In the attempt to stress the behavioral traits that underlie true worship of God, both the prophets and Yeshua repeatedly deemphasized the traditional tendency of adhering to rite and ritual as an end by itself. They objected to all forms of rite and ritual that did not give first place to loving care, the primary religious obligation.

A classic example is the criticism that Yeshua—citing Isaiah and Hosea before him—leveled against the interpretation given by some religious leaders of the binding power of vows. According to a custom of the time, lay devotees made vows and set apart money for their fulfillment. According to some traditions at the time, the money so set apart could not be used even in case of a family emergency, such as the sudden illness of a father or mother. Criticizing such interpretation of the worship of God, Yeshua said: "Hypocrites, it was you Isaiah meant when he rightly prophesied: 'Those people honor me with their lips, while their hearts are far from me. The worship they offer is useless. The doctrines they teach are only human regulations'" (Matt. 15:7-9). Like the prophets before him and the Rabbis after him, even sacrifice was not what was important to Yeshua: "If you would have under stood the meaning of the words, 'what I want is mercy, not sacrifice,' you would not have condemned the blameless" (Matt. 12:7).

The very observance of the Sabbath, which was the most obligatory religious practice of the time, was of lesser importance for Yeshua than was caring for the needy. He once said: "The Sabbath was made for human beings, and not human beings for the Sabbath" (Mark 2:27), much as another rabbi elsewhere said: "The Sabbath is committed to you; you are not committed to the Sabbath' I (*Mekilta*, 31. 13, 14 [Smith, 1381). Ritualistic washing or paying of tithes to the temple were equally secondary, as with Isaiah quoted earlier: "You offer your tithe of all sorts of garden-herbs, and overlook justice and love of God" (Luke 1, 1:42).

In examining the critical attitude of the prophets and Yeshua, and many of his fellow Jews, there is revealed a common bond between Gautama on the one hand, and the prophets and Yeshua on the other, in the stand each of them took against the theism of their day. Unanimously, they condemned the false theism that prevailed in the societies to which they belonged. The prophets, Yeshua, and his fellow Jews, of course, did not go so far as Gautama in completely rejecting the idea of God, but all were at one in their conviction that there is an utterly meaningless form of theism that is destructive to the personality. They were at one in affirming that the best and the most needed form of the worship of God is that expressed by sublimity of character or a life of goodness.

Chapter Seventeen

Worship of God: Its Inner Reality

The fact that the prophets and Yeshua pointed out a wrong worship of God in their societies, and openly denounced it, is a datum of great help in any comparative study. It reduces considerably the distance between the theism of the Judeo-Christian tradition and the non-theism of Buddhism.

But it alone cannot resolve the problem of disparity, for no one can deny the fact that, after all, the idea of God is central and not just peripheral to Yeshua's thought and to Judaism and Christianity. If we are to solve this problem in some substantial way, we have to go a step further and look for the inner reality behind belief in God. In other words, we have to catch sight of the deep human experience that corresponds to the traditional externalized form of divine worship.

Conceptualization and Experience

The first step is to recognize that there are two levels, and not just one, in which humanity reaches out to divinity. One is the level of concept; the other, the level of experience. Of these, the one that is almost exclusively taken into account in traditional theology is the first. But for the effective comparison of a theistic religion with a nontheistic one, relying on that way alone can lead one nowhere.

Jews and Christians, therefore, who want to compare Buddhism with Christianity and Judaism should start by examining their own belief in God. That is the only way for them to discover its inner core. In other words, they should start by submitting their own *concept* of God to an impartial critical analysis. Simple as it

147

may sound, this is an exercise that calls for a certain courage and broadmindedness. If they do so, they will discover to their amazement that their own *concept* of God, which until then they would have considered something unique, is just one amidst a variety of concepts of God found in society today. Many others who today worship God or gods have concepts of divinity very different from that of the Christian and the Jew. Some concepts found in India, for example, may be mentioned as illustrations.

God can be male (Krishna) or female (Parvati). The idea of a mother goddess was a very popular belief in ancient India. A god can be married; Vishnu is married to Lakshmi. He may have one wife or several wives; god Katarangama has two wives. A god can be pictured as having several heads and hands (Sivanataraja) or as a human being with some animal features. The god Ganesha is shown as having an elephant face, and the god Hanuman, a monkey face. God can be a person or an impersonal reality. The *Atman-Brahman*, or the world-soul of the Hindus, is impersonal.

The Judeo-Christian idea of God may present a more evolved and more refined version of God, but still it remains only one among many ways in which humanity pictures to itself the unseen, unheard transcendental Reality.

Anthropomorphic picturization (i.e., illustration of unseen reality using pictures of human behavior) is the only way in which a human being can "conceptualize" (i.e., form a concept of) something that is not an object of the senses. If the transcendental reality is to be conceptualized, then picturization, on a pattern jointly accepted by a group, is the only solution.

Christians and Jews too must realize that their concept of God, even when God is thought of as a spirit, is only a picturization. According to their picture God is a person, a father, a mother.[11] God is a forgiver, a creator (maker), a king with a kingdom. God is a judge, a rewarder, a punisher, who talks (in revelation), listens (in prayer), is offended (when humans sin). In any discussion on theism and atheism, Jews and Christians should never forget that their concept of God is thus composed of pictures borrowed from behavioral patterns of human beings, and that its inner content is more complex than they ordinarily take it to be. There is probably no concept more difficult to analyze than that of God. Whitehead is quite right when he says:

> Today there is but one religious dogma in debate: What do you mean by "God"? In this respect, today is like all yesterdays. This is the fundamental religious dogma, and all other dogmas are subsidiary to it [Whitehead, 68].

And as Paul Tillich points out so well, the problem is rooted in the human action of conceptualization. The human concept does not represent the reality fully:

> The word "God" produces a contradiction in the consciousness. It involves something figurative that is present in the consciousness, and something not figurative. In the word "God" is contained, at the same time, that which actually functions as a representation, and also the peculiarity of transcending its own conceptual content [Tillich, 13].

The only way to resolve this "contradiction," therefore, is carefully to distinguish between what is figurative—the concept—and what is not figurative—the experience. Further, it must be remembered that the general concept of God is composed of several sub-concepts. To discover what is implied by the term "God" we must define the experiential dimension of each of the sub-concepts.

The following analysis is not intended as a complete explanation of the experience involved, but it could well be a starting point for one who wishes to discover the human experience that is conceptualized under the term God.

Concept: God as Creator of the Universe and of Humankind

Experience (behavior). In an adult way, persons see themselves as beings with limited power. Their contact with human realities such as sickness and death convinces them that they do not have total dominion over themselves. They *accept their finitude* as their human condition.

Looking at themselves from another angle, they realize that they are part of the Universe. *They are related to all that is in the Universe*-the sun, the moon, the stars, trees, animals, fire, water, air. Like a leaf that is part of the tree, in spite of their individual identities they realize that still they are integral parts of the Universe.

Even when they witness destructive incidents in the Universe, such as floods, droughts, earthquakes, conflagrations, they do not lose sight of the intrinsic beauty, power, and goodness of the Universe. They see that the Universe is in *the process of growth and development, and that the progress of the world follows a purpose and a plan*.

Even their personal deaths they see as part of that great life-uplifting plan, and so the certainty of death does not frighten them. For them death is as much endowed with purpose as birth. They may, of course, not comprehend that purpose fully, or for that matter, anything beyond birth and death. They may even be aware that their death will be as much beyond their determining power as their birth had been. *Those limitations do not frustrate them, for they are sure that death is not a termination that makes life futile*. As far as they are concerned, they are thankful that they now have sufficient intelligence and control over themselves to bring their lives into full maturity.

Maturity at any level of life is endowed with a life-saving power. Maturity saves a living being from its inner life-destructive elements. A grain of wheat that is ripe or mature, unlike one that is not, is a potential plant assured of regenerated life. It does not

150

disappear when it disintegrates into the earth. What is true of maturity in vegetative life is in a higher though less visualizable way true of maturity in the life of the mind or the spirit. A fully mature individual enjoys a resurrected or revitalized form of life. A resurrected life does not necessarily mean a life that *follows* physical death. It is a life lived *regardless* of death. It is primarily a triumph over spiritual death or mental immaturity.

For mature adults, survival in its fuller sense is connected with humanly realizable mental maturity, rather than with the idea of a static, non-maturing "soul." In the vegetative life, of course, maturity is totally given by the forces of nature. In conscious life, or the life of the spirit, it is achieved by one's own efforts under the gracious support of the life-giving powers of the Universe. Human maturity is thus both a liberation and a salvation; both an achievement and a gift.

Concept: God as Father/Mother

Experience. Persons realize that in the worst crises of life-poverty, sickness, failure in family life-they are not alone or abandoned. They live their lives with a feeling that they are wanted and that they are loved. *Their feeling of oneness with the Universe gives them a feeling of security.* They know that the forces of the Universe are always behind them to help them. Medical science has shown that the power of healing injuries and sickness is in Nature itself, and that medicine, by removing infections, only helps the curative processes of Nature. Accordingly, they realize that the healing and the protective powers of the Universe are with them. As long as they do not isolate themselves from the Universe through a false attitude of self-sufficiency, they know that they can enjoy its life-giving power.

They accept, too, their relationship with the whole of humankind. *They take every human being as their brother and sister as if they had all a common mother/father.* They are concerned about them. They care for them. They are ready to

151

undergo any inconvenience to secure for any underprivileged person or group the opportunity for a life with dignity.

Concept: God as Judge

Experience. Persons have the intuitive conviction that qualities such as patience, generosity, and concern for others upgrade them, give them a higher qualitative existence, whereas attitudes such as hatred, envy, pride, and dishonesty downgrade them. They realize that every action of theirs has to be motivated by a sense of responsibility toward life and the universe in its entirety. And for them, to be responsible is to be accountable. They believe that true and lasting joy comes from a life of service and that the pleasure resulting from selfish sense-satisfaction is short-lived.

The actions by which persons express their worship of God represent in a similar way their particular attitude toward themselves, the many forms of life in the world, the society in which they live, and the world at large.

Concept: Adoration of God

Experience. Persons look at themselves without false pride or a false sense of superiority. They accept the paradox of life, that a certain selflessness is what makes them discover their true Self. They are ready to sacrifice personal pleasures and possessions on the altar of duty and generosity. They are ready to suffer for the welfare of others.

Concept: Praise of God

Experience. Persons experience a sense of wonderment before the harmony, beauty, and goodness of the world around them. Their sense of admiration is such that even in a criminal they see an inner goodness; in the trials that befall them they see a meaning. They are so joyful that they never let themselves fall into despair or frustration.

Concept: Petition to God

Experience. In moments of trial and difficulty persons soon recover from resultant anxiety and fear by reestablishing their harmony with the Universe. This reunification with the powers of the Universe helps them to gather up their courage and go forward in the steadfast pursuit of their aims in life.

Concept: Repentance and Forgiveness

Experience. Persons look at their own mistakes and correct themselves. They are not ashamed of their failings. Even when society rejects them for those failings, they do not reject themselves; even if society condemns them, they know that Nature does not. They accept others with *their* failings. They are ready to forgive them "seventy times seven" times.

Conceptually Nontheistic Belief in God

The patterns of human behavior described above, corresponding to different elements of belief in God, are by no means fully exhaustive. Further, they are based on the Judeo-Christian tradition and may not necessarily correspond to the Buddhist spiritual experience.

Nevertheless, the above analysis could illustrate an important truth about belief in God. It shows that there could be an acknowledgment of God even where there is no *concept* of God. There can be a sanctity that is *conceptually* non-theistic.

Whether an individual holds the concept or not, faith in God really refers to a person's higher mental attitude toward self, life, society, and the Universe. This is well expressed in the reflection upon his own faith by Dr. John Cobb in his booklet, *To Pray or Not to Pray*:

> As I have reflected on what this distinctively Christian understanding of God means for Christian spiritual life, I have been led to understand it quite

153

differently. I find God in the natural processes of my body, when these are not thwarted and impeded by external interferences. I find God in my feelings, when these are open and spontaneous. I find God in my imagination when this is free and creative. I find God in my will when it aims at justice and righteousness. I find God in my spirit when it orients the whole of my life towards that which is worth achieving and frees me from petty self-serving concerns [Cobb, 17].

Thus, true belief in God is basically a special pattern of human behavior and not primarily a matter of *concept*. There is, of course, an objection that any traditional Jew or Christian will be compelled to raise against this analysis of the notion of God. Is God *only* that? Is an adult human attitude the only thing to be understood as corresponding to the term "God"? Is God not also an external objective reality? Is there no being apart from human beings rightly thought of as Creator, Father/Mother, and who is to be adored, praised, and thanked?

This is a very human question, but very incorrectly posed. The question here is not whether an outside objective reality exists or not. The question is how this reality is apprehended by the mind. Is God apprehended through conceptualization or through experience? Is God a conceptualized reality that is experienced? Or an experienced reality that is conceptualized?

This is not to say that concepts of God as a supra-human being are altogether harmful and therefore to be totally rejected. When it comes to *thinking about* God, we *have to* form concepts, just as we must for contemplating any reality that is not sensorial.

Further, conceptualization serves many practical purposes. First, it is helpful when individuals communicate with others. Experience is too personal to be communicated directly and must be objectivized and picturized. Secondly, in situations such as the teaching of religion to children, a conceptualized version of God is very necessary. A child can grasp experience only through visual aids. We should also never forget that the "child" continues to survive in the most adult person, which explains the common adult preference for a conceptualized version of God.

But persons who are intellectually mature should never fail to realize the weak side of a concept when used in reference to God. Divinity in its deeper form can in no way be visualized. It can only be experienced.

They should also not fail to see that the place where persons experience divinity is within their own selves, and the moment they do so is when they discover their own true selves. But, paradoxical as it may sound, persons discover their true selves only when they get out of their "selves" to live a life of selflessness.

Selflessness may have different modes of expression, and different modes may be accentuated by different religions. But, whatever be the mode of expression, when the Judeo-Christian idea of belief in God is taken in its deeper dimensions, there is not the least doubt that the most authentic way of acknowledging God is a life of selflessness. Judaism and Christianity in that sense, just as much as Buddhism, are an "a-selfish," "an-individualistic" form of human experience. If that is so, have we not to think anew about the 4 'atheism" of Gautama? Have we not to say that Buddhism is atheistic only in reference to belief in God taken in its imperfect, conceptualized sense?

Chapter Eighteen

Liberation according to Gautama, Yeshua, and Judaism

As the two preceding chapters should have shown, when seen against their historical background, Gautama's atheism and Judeo-Christian theism are not two attitudes antagonistic to each other. Both have one common aim: to awaken persons to a sense of realism and responsibility in their day-to-day life.

This non-antagonism by itself, however, cannot prove much. It cannot, for example, indicate with sufficient precision whether Buddhism, Judaism, and Christianity are in fact interiorly related, and if so, how closely they are. For that we have to go a step further and inquire whether Yeshua and his fellow Jews understood religion and liberation exactly as Gautama did—in other words, whether the main concern of Yeshua and Judaism was also the transformation of the inner personality of the human being.

In the search for the right answer, Christians and Jews here are bound to meet with a preliminary difficulty. The word "liberation" does not figure as prominently in the language of Judaism and Yeshua as in that of Gautama. The reason for that is not difficult to find. Gautama inherited from the Indian background a clear intellectual preoccupation with the idea of liberation (*moksha, vimukti*). Liberation was a theme commonly discussed among Indian thinkers from very ancient times. In that regard Judaism and Yeshua were less fortunate. At the time of Yeshua, and of Hillel, Akiba, and the other founding Rabbis of Judaism, not only was liberation left out of philosophical speculation, it even had a different connotation, a political one.

The problem that the Israelites as a people had often faced was the threat of foreign invasion. Hence when they spoke of liberation, they often thought of it primarily as liberation from political slavery-as in the historic exodus from Egypt. Further, in their God-centered thinking pattern, they assumed that God alone could achieve it for them. That is why they used the word "salvation" in preference to the term "liberation." Salvation is liberation insofar as it is achieved for one by another. Of course, there were Jewish educators—the prophets, Yeshua, and later the Rabbis—who tried to purify this idea of salvation, and to give it a correct religious dimension but, on the whole, the term tended to remain complex and rather mixed.

Perhaps this explains why the term "salvation"—as well as "liberation"—is hardly ever used by Yeshua. What he used by preference is the term "reign of God" or "reign of heaven." The two phrases are synonymous, the latter in keeping with a pious Jewish custom in use to this day of avoiding utterance of the name of God. Hence the rabbinic Hebrew term is *malkut shomaim*, the "reign of the heavens," and the New Testament Greek translation of it is *basileia ton ouranon* (the New Testament writers also sometimes avoided the pious euphemism and used the "reign of God," *basileia tou theou*).

As careful scholarship has painstakingly discerned:

> Jesus of Nazareth was not the first to speak of the kingdom of God. Nor was John the Baptist.... Both proclaim that it is near. This presupposes that it was already known to the first hearers, their Jewish contemporaries. This concrete link is decisive. It gives us a positive relationship of Jesus and the Baptist with apocalyptic and the Rabbinic writings [Schmidt, I, 584].

Therefore, in speaking of the reign of God, Yeshua was talking of the *malkut shomaim* of the other Rabbis before and after him, and they all meant basically the same thing by it: the rule of God, a condition wherein all things were ordered according to God's rule or "reign."

The term "reign of God" is one that Jewish and Christian students will have to explore to find out whether Gautama's notion of liberation was common to Judaism and Yeshua too. Unfortunately, it is a notion whose meaning is not self-evident to moderns. As an image, it says much less to the person of today than to the Jew of Yeshua's era. In a society such as ours, in which autocracies have been replaced by democracies, kings and kingdoms are no longer be literary figures or images that communicate much. But if the barrier caused by the distance of time could overcome, and we could recapture the sense in which it was originally used, we would automatically be led to conclude that the "reign" of Judaism and Yeshua was not very different from the *nirvana* of Gautama.

That abrupt statement of course could cause a certain dismay to someone who hears it for the first time. The identification or even the approximation of nirvana with the reign of God could shock the Buddhist as well as the Jew and the Christian. This is because these terms are very sacred to each. Nirvana for Buddhists, and the reign of God for Jews and Christians represent the ultimate goal of life that each group aspires to in its own specific way. Therefore Buddhists, Jews, and Christians cannot be blamed if they consider their own goal so unique that they resent its being compared to another.

But probably a greater reason behind the fear of any such comparison is that the two terms are no longer taken by the majority in the sense in which they were originally intended. Both these terms have been victims of similar corruption in meaning in the course of centuries and at the hands of popular, unintrospective preachers. As a result, in the mind of the ordinary Buddhist, Jew, and Christian, nirvana and the reign of God have nothing to do with the mental awakening of a person. For the large majority of Buddhists, Jews, and Christians, nirvana and the reign are realities that are approached exclusively through the doorway of death. "May he (she) attain *nirvana*" is the wish of the Buddhist with

158

reference to a deceased person. "May the angels of God take her (him) to heaven (or the kingdom of God)" is the natural wish of Christians and Jews when they assist at a funeral.

But in the original usage of Gautama, the Rabbis, and Yeshua, nirvana and the reign of God are realities that pertain primarily to an individual's life here and now. They designate the fullness of the humanhood that individuals can achieve at this moment. They both describe the state of mind of fully awakened individuals or of persons fully liberated from their personality weaknesses.

The fact that both these terms refer to an identical human reality does not of course mean that there is no difference whatsoever between them. Analysis of a human reality originating in two cultures so different from each other as the Jewish and the Indian could not be identical in every detail. But what we must not fail to realize is that those differences do not touch what is essential or central to the notion, but only secondary or peripheral aspects.

For instance, some of the parables used by the Rabbis and Yeshua to illustrate the reign of God show that they thought of the reign not only on the level of personality but also on the level of building a new society. If individuals were rightly transformed, the Rabbis and Yeshua foresaw that a new, righteous society would someday arise. They looked forward to it, and through their ministry wanted to pave the way for it. Nonetheless their main preoccupation was not so much the building up of new structures for a new society, as the building up of new citizens for that society.

In the same way, their idea of the reign of God accommodated within it the popular Jewish belief in a life beyond death. But the fact that they held that belief does not mean that what they understood first and foremost by the reign was *just* another life after death. To think so would be a gross misrepresentation of their teaching.

There is of course no doubt that they exploited to the full the Jewish belief of a judgment by God after death or at the "end of the world." Like any good educator, the Rabbis and Yeshua used such popular beliefs to bring out more forcefully the validity of good actions performed here and now. In their hands, the image of a divine judgment served the same purpose as a measuring weight does in the hands of a merchant. He puts a publicly approved measuring weight on one side of his scales to show the value or the heaviness of the merchandise that he puts on the other side. What both the merchant and the consumer are primarily interested in is the merchandise so weighed and not the measuring weight as such.

Thus, for any perceptive inquirer, the reign of God taught by the Rabbis and Yeshua has to do with life after death only secondarily. In spite of the popular Jewish imagery adopted by them, their doctrine of the reign did not say anything more about afterlife than did Gautama's doctrine of *nirvana*. The reign referred primarily to the quality of life of an individual who has evolved from childish to adult behavior.

Even though there is no doubt as to the principal sense in which the Rabbis and Yeshua used the reign of God image, we cannot escape the fact that for simple Christians and Jews of today, who live in a totally different social context, the image itself appears somewhat foreign and blurred. And so, they cannot be totally blamed if they attribute a greater importance to its secondary aspects and tend generally to interpret it as a place to go to after death. Therefore, all told, it is not prudent for comparative students to depend exclusively on the reign image when they want to find out whether the Rabbis and Yeshua had the same understanding of human liberation as did Gautama. It is wiser on those students' part to take the main doctrines that Yeshua and the Rabbis preached and to look at the objective they strove to achieve by that preaching. Whatever they preached, when introspectively examined, it will be seen to have been preached with a single ultimate objective in view. This objective was none other than the curing of the inner ailments which human beings were suffering from and which were consequently the fundamental obstacles to a life of authentic human nobility and happiness.

Three doctrines that deserve to be examined in this regard, particularly because they pertain to the essence of both Judaism and Christianity equally, are: 1) the doctrine of faith in a provident God, 2) the doctrine of the forgiveness of sins, and 3) the doctrine of love of neighbor, or human interrelatedness.

Faith in a Provident God

Through their insight into concrete human nature, Yeshua and the Rabbis clearly saw that many persons were unable to accept adult responsibility in life and act as free, noble beings because they were interiorly thwarted by feelings of inner anxiety and despair. As is equally evident today, countless daily problems bring about psychological breakdowns. Desertion of a friend, criticism from a companion, illness, the threat of hunger and financial destitution are instances. Any such problem can drain out energy from persons and rob them of their enthusiasm, making them completely incapable of facing the problems before them. As a result of such obsessive feelings they come to a state of despair in which they tell themselves, "No, I cannot," "I am finished," "There is nothing more I can do."

It was to redeem humanity from such a devastating state of mental depression that the Rabbis and Yeshua taught the doctrine of faith in a provident God:

> This is why I am telling you not to worry about your life and what you are to eat, nor about your body and how you are to clothe it.... Look at the birds in the sky, they do not sow nor reap nor gather into barns. Yet your Heavenly Father feeds them. And see again how beautifully God clothes the grass in the field which is here today and thrown into the furnace tomorrow. Will he not much more look after you, you of little faith? [Matt. 6:25-30].

161

Did you ever in your life see an animal or a bird which had a trade? And they support themselves without trouble. And were they not created only to serve me? And I was created to serve my master. Does it not follow that I shall be supported without trouble? [*Kiddushin*, 4.14 (Smith, 137)].

This doctrine of the providence of God, or "faith," *emmunah*, as Yeshua and the Rabbis termed it, is one that is easily misinterpreted. If it is not to be misunderstood, it must be seen in the light of the motive with which it was preached, which was psychological in nature. One who is unable to recognize the damage that despair causes in the life of a human being cannot properly appreciate the real value of faith.

Then again, to understand it correctly, one has to go beyond the anthropomorphic dress in which it is clothed. When shorn of its anthropomorphic coat, faith in a protecting God is quite a rationally tenable doctrine. It says that in the worst circumstances of life, humans have no reason to feel weak. Weakness results from a false belief that we are isolated beings totally abandoned to ourselves. The doctrine of a provident God reminds them that in reality they are part of the Universe, always linked with it, and constantly sustained by its powers. No individuals, for example, could live for a moment if the sun did not provide the necessary light and warmth, if the air around them did not provide the required oxygen, and if the force of gravity did not keep their bodies in balance. The Universe has more resources of energy than are known to us and as long as we do not block the flow of their power into ourselves we can harness their life-supporting, problem-solving energy for self-preservation and personality growth. Through the doctrine of providence, Yeshua and the Rabbis, as it were, said to the depressed: have faith, and keep united with the life-giving energy of the Universe. It is within you and is waiting to revitalize you.

Thus, faith in a provident God can be looked at as a technique that the Rabbis and Yeshua used to cure persons of a very common mental sickness. A widespread sickness of human beings is lack of

162

self-confidence. Due to an unrealistic view of themselves and of life in general, many constantly succumb to a feeling of helplessness. Strange as it may sound, the Rabbis and Yeshua here used the very doctrine of belief in God as a medicine to awaken in women and men a belief in themselves.

Forgiveness by God

To cure humanity of another equally widespread mental sickness, Yeshua and the Rabbis preached the doctrine of divine forgiveness. To understand realistically the salvific value of forgiveness, we must be able to visualize the extensiveness of the psychological damage that guilt feelings cause in a person.

Sin and guilt are not identical realities, though the latter often follows the former. Sin is the act of violating a moral law. Guilt is the judgment of self-condemnation that ensues as a result. Awareness of sin is something good; it accompanies adult sensitivity to obligations and duties in life. Guilt feelings, on the other hand, are harmful. They drive persons to despair, and take away from them the very possibility of reforming themselves. *Guilt feelings* arise in persons because they are not mature enough to realize that moral failings are not exclusive to them, and that they are—however unfortunate it may be—the common lot of the whole of humankind. None of us is born a perfect being, a mature adult; we have to grow into it by persistently rising from falls.

Most religious persons have spoken against sin, but perhaps no one has paid so much attention to its guilt dimensions as did Yeshua and the Rabbis. Religion teachers, due to their unacquaintance with the torturous nature of guilt, ordinarily refer only to punishment when they speak of sin. Yeshua and the Rabbis, however, stress forgiveness when they speak of sin.

Yeshua's doctrine of forgiveness is enshrined in his parable traditionally referred to as the parable of the prodigal son, but which, more meaningfully, should be called the parable of the

163

prodigal father (Luke 15:11-22). According to that story the youngest son in a family decided all on his own to break away from the father, take his share of the family inheritance, and go off to a distant land in search of worldly thrills. Not long after his departure, he made a mess of his life, and realized the folly of his decision. In the resultant state of utter helplessness, he decided to go back home.

One would have expected the father of such a breakaway son to have disowned the son on his departure, and to have thrown him out on his return. But not so, this father. From the day of the son's departure, he yearned for his return, and when he did return, he welcomed him back with open arms.

The same point, with almost identical images, was made by several rabbinical parables, such as the following:

> It is like a king's son who fell into a bad way of life. The king sent his tutor to him and had him say: Come back, my son! But the son said: How can I go back in this situation since I am ashamed before you. His father had said to him: My son, can there be a son who is ashamed to return to his father? If you return, do you not return to your father? Thus, God also sent Jeremiah to the Israelites [Rabbah on Deut. 4:30 (Billerbeck, II, 216)].

The benevolent father in the stories is, according to Yeshua and the Rabbis, the ever-forgiving God. Through those stories Yeshua and the Rabbis sought to console those ridden with guilt feelings, saying to them that God, the universal source of goodness, does not reject them, so they must not reject themselves.

Forgiveness is a doctrine that many have found difficult to approve. Many ask whether forgiveness is not an encouragement to further sinning. Such persons consider the doctrine of forgiveness to be unjust and antireligious, particularly because it seems to ignore and disregard the goodness of the virtuous. In the story of the prodigal son, that attitude is taken by the older son. He objected to the openhearted, forgiving attitude of his father.

According to Yeshua, those who do not permit others to be forgiven live under an illusion about themselves. Those who easily pass judgment on others are often concealing a guilty conscience. The religious leaders who brought to Yeshua a woman taken in adultery and who wanted her stoned were doing exactly that. With the intention of unmasking them, Yeshua declared: "Let whoever is without sin cast the first stone" (John 8:9). According to Yeshua even those who appeared virtuous were sinners at heart and had no right to object to the offer of forgiveness extended to those suffering from guilt.

As in the doctrine of providence, a *concept* of God is not basic to an understanding of forgiveness. As much as in the doctrine of providence, in the doctrine of forgiveness too, the concept of God is anthropomorphic and based on the Jewish concept of God at the time. The image of a forgiving human father is transferred to God. The purpose of Yeshua and the Rabbis, however, was not to draw a picture of God, but to lead individuals to a better understanding of human nature and ultimately to a correct sense of self-acceptance.

Modern psychologists who are able to break through the shell of anthropomorphic language attach increasing therapeutic value to the Judeo-Christian doctrine of forgiveness. According to them every individual in an un-adult stage is a split personality. The emotional self and the intuitive self are torn apart from each other, and are at war with each other. Forgiveness represents the state in which the intuitive self assures the emotional self: "You are accepted by me." The split caused in the personality by the sense of guilt is thereby healed. The person so reintegrated and restored can thereafter resume a good life unperturbed by the contempt that society may show her or him. Forgiveness by God is the religious expression of the psychological doctrine of self-acceptance. Forgiveness is a doctrine of healing.

The doctrine of divine forgiveness and that of divine providence show how different the Rabbis' and Yeshua's attitude as educators is from that of popular preachers of righteousness. The popular preacher speaks only of the moral standards that an individual should follow. The Rabbis and Yeshua also spoke of moral standards, and of very high moral standards at that. But they did not begin there or stop there. They saw in humans, certain intrinsic obstacles that made it nearly impossible for them to keep to such moral standards. Humans were victims of feelings of self-diffidence and self-rejection. Yeshua and the Rabbis felt that ordinary humans should first be redeemed from such weaknesses if they were to carry out adult responsibilities successfully. That is why they taught so emphatically the doctrines of providence and forgiveness.

Human Interrelatedness

There was, according to Yeshua and the Rabbis, a third deficiency in humans that prevented them from living up to their adult responsibilities. It was their blindness to their state of inner oneness with other human beings. Immature adults, due to a very childish view of themselves and of life, think that the only way to achieve true greatness is to live exclusively for themselves. The Rabbis and Yeshua show that such an attitude destroys its very goal.

Human beings are by essence interrelated beings, and they cannot be full human beings if they do not live and practice that interrelatedness. There are three beautiful parables or image stories that Yeshua—paralleled in at least one instance by other Rabbis—used to educate his listeners on this point.

The first is the story of Dives, the rich man, and Lazarus, the beggar (Luke 16:19-3 1).[12] Dives lived a life of luxury. He draped himself in rich clothes. He ate and drank sumptuously. At the entrance to his gate was a poor beggar, Lazarus, sick and covered with sores. His only food was the crumbs of bread thrown away from the rich man's table, and brought to him by the rich man's

166

servants. The story ends with the picture of what happens to these two after their death. Lazarus is in heaven and Dives in hell.

The lesson that Yeshua tried to put across through this story is a very powerful one. There was nothing in the behavior of the rich man that, according to popular assessment, could justify his being condemned to eternal hell fire. There was nothing immoral in his life. He did not kill, steal, or commit adultery. He did not even harm the poor man at the gate. He did not kick him as he passed by, or throw him out. And after all, what is wrong in a person's enjoying a good life, particularly if blessed with a rich inheritance? But Yeshua says Dives was guilty, and so gravely guilty as to merit condemnation to eternal hell fire. His only crime was that he ignored the poor man at the gate. He was unconcerned about the helplessness of persons in his immediate environment.

No adult or responsible person, according to Yeshua, can be unconcerned about the needy. Human beings are truly human only to the extent that they live up to their nature related, as it is, to other human beings.

Yeshua's second story is equally powerful. It has been referred to earlier. It is the story of the good Samaritan (Luke 10:25-37). There are three characters in the story—a priest, a Levite, and a Samaritan. The first two characters are symbols of accepted religious piety. The third is a religiously impure outcaste. All of them meet a helpless person, fallen by the wayside, a victim of brigands. The first two see the victim, and pass by. The "non-religious" Samaritan alone comes to the rescue. In contrast to the first two, Yeshua pointed to the Samaritan as the truly religious person, the only adult in the group.

The third story is the one built around the Jewish belief in a final judgment at the end of the world. Yeshua uses that popular image to show what true adulthood in the present life is. Those who according to the story were judged to be deserving of the reward of heaven were those who had lived correctly their life of interrelatedness and cared for those in need. The judge says to them:

The sayings of other Rabbis carried much the same thought and similar language:

> And so, the Holy One, blessed be He, said to Israel, "My Children, whenever you feed the poor I count it up for you as if you fed me" [*Midrash Tannaim* 15 (Smith, 154)].

If the imagery of Yeshua and the Rabbis is correctly understood, all these three love-of-neighbor stories will be seen to teach one simple lesson. Humans essentially are related beings. If they are truly to be humans, they must express in their lives that interrelatedness or neighborliness by a life of concern for others. Charity is not just a meritorious action that one is free to do or not to do. Only a person concerned about others deserves to be called fully human, a religious human being.

Of these three teachings of the Rabbis and Yeshua—providence, forgiveness, and inte-rrelatedness—the last, as will be readily granted, is not exclusive to the Judeo-Christian tradition. It is found in Buddhism too. Loving kindness or *maitriya* (literally, "friendliness") is for Gautama an indispensable characteristic of the adult human being.

The doctrines of providence and forgiveness are not found in the same form in Buddhism. But it is not impossible that the sense of realism they represent is contained in a different form in Buddhism. Gautama's teaching on Right Understanding, for example, is deep enough to embrace the message underlying even those doctrines.

The purpose of the above analysis, however, is not to prove that the Rabbis, Yeshua, and Gautama taught the same thing or even that they conceived of the process of personality transformation exactly in the same way. In fact, they may well have looked at the various

168

elements of that process differently. They may well have viewed immaturity (*samsara*, kingdom of the devil) in different ways. They may have understood the stature of the adulthood (arahatship and *nirvana*, or sainthood and reign of God) that an individual is to aspire to in different ways. They may have even resorted to different techniques in their attempt to effect that inner transformation. In fact, the techniques they resorted to were different. Gautama relied mostly on the notion of the no-self to awaken persons to a sense of realism about life. Yeshua and the Rabbis used the doctrines of forgiveness and providence.

Whatever the diversities were with regard to such aspects, the ultimate goal of religion and religious liberation was the same for all: the development of the human person. For none of them was religion, as it is for many persons today, just a matter of fidelity to religious practices or traditions. Nor was it for them just a matter of a happy life after death.

The single-mindedness of Gautama, the Rabbis, and Yeshua with regard to the aim of religion easily leads to the conclusion that there is a strong *inner* affinity between Buddhism, Judaism, and Christianity. Even the fact that Judaism and Christianity are theistic and Buddhism non-theistic does not minimize in any way the unity of vision that Gautama, Yeshua, and the Rabbis had with regard to the nature of religion and its primary function.

Epilogue

I sincerely hope that the preceding pages have given Jewish and Christian readers an acquaintance with Buddhism both in itself, and in comparison with Christianity and Judaism. Such an acquaintance should also help them to rediscover Judaism and Christianity in a better light.

Not long ago it was maintained that a Christian's and a Jew's study of another religion would be harmful to their respective faiths. Any religion apart from Judaism or Christianity was considered "pagan," and contact with it was to be avoided. That extreme view does not prevail any longer. But the age-old Jewish and Christian unconcern for other religions and philosophies is not totally dead. For many, the study of another religion, even though not harmful, is not a necessity. At best, it is a worthwhile pursuit for those who have the time for it.

But I like to think with Whitehead that it is something not only very useful but even necessary. It is necessary for the progress and purification of Christianity and Judaism. With reference to a Christian's or a Jew's study of Buddhism (and vice versa) an observation made by Whitehead can serve as an eye-opener in this regard. Though it explicitly speaks of just Christianity, it is equally applicable to the entire Judeo-Christian tradition:

> The decay of Christianity and Buddhism, as determinative influences in modern thought, is partly due to the fact that each religion has unduly sheltered itself from the other. The self-sufficient pedantry of learning and the confidence of ignorant zealots have combined to shut up each religion in its own forms of thought. Instead of looking to each other for deeper meanings, they have remained self-satisfied and unfertilized [Whitehead, 140].

170

The study just completed should become a little more meaningful if seen in the light of this reflection.

Because this exposition is primarily meant for Christians and Jews, I have followed in it an approach rather uncommon to many general books on Buddhism. Most books on Buddhism are concerned almost exclusively with what is contained in it or with what Gautama taught. The *what* of a religion is of course very important for an understanding of that religion. But the *what* alone is not sufficient.

To fully understand the thought of the founders of religions one has also to discover *why* they taught what they did. The aim that particular religious founders strove to attain is as important for the understanding of the religion as their teachings themselves. It is because they had particular aims that they taught particular doctrines rather than others.

The existence of a *why* or aim behind the *what* or content of a pronouncement is not something that is exclusive to matters of religion. It is true in any field where a liberation of some form is implied. Medicine is a good case in point. A doctor's prescription, for example, has both a *what* and a *why*. To a patient suffering, say, from an internal ulcer, one doctor (a physician) could prescribe oral drugs, and another (a surgeon) surgery. The *what* of those two treatment plans is very different, but their *why* is identical. Both treatment plans have as their aim the curing of the ulcer.

According to Buddhism, and in fact according to all religions of Indian origin, religious doctrines are necessarily only prescriptions aimed at restoring health in an ailing person. Bereft of that liberational goal, a religious doctrine has no value at all. From the point of view of those religions, the value of a doctrine is not so much in its veracity as in its effectiveness. A religious doctrine is not so much to be accepted as to be applied.

That is why religions of Indian origin are hardly ever concerned with dogmas and dogmatic definitions. Even heresies are no

171

problem to them. Heresies are only opinions. Sects too could exist among them, but sects are not mutually exclusive. Indian religions look for a *why* beneath the *what* of any doctrine. The *why*, furthermore, is for them the element that determines the *what*.

The fact that there is a *why* beneath the *what* of every doctrine is not a matter that could be said to have caught the attention of Christians very much. The same is true for Jews regarding the *why* beneath the *what* of various of their traditional practices. Coming to an awareness of that fact may very likely be one of the first benefits that Christians and Jews would gain from a study of Buddhism.

A Christian and a Jew who are ready to accept that there is a *why* beneath the *what* of religious teachings and traditional customs are sure to see Buddhism, and particularly the relationship between Buddhism, Judaism, and Christianity, in a totally new light. There is not the least doubt that, judged exteriorly, Buddhism, Judaism, and Christianity are very different from each other. The *what* of each of them is almost irreconcilably different. But deep beneath their *what* is a *why* that to a great extent is identical. Anybody who digs deeply enough to discover the *why* of the three religious traditions will come to the place where s/he will see the three traditions bound together by a strong *inner* affinity.

To see a religion in terms of its *why* is naturally to see it in terms of its primary function, or better, its mission. If there is an affinity between Judaism, Christianity, and Buddhism with regard to their mission, then an important question is bound to arise with regard to the fulfillment of that mission, or in other words, with regard to missionary work: What is the responsibility of Christian missionaries who come to realize that there could be an affinity between their work and that of Buddhist missionaries? The same issue is also of fundamental concern to Judaism, for it too was a missionary religion well into the Common Era and is becoming so again under the leadership of the Reform Movement in the United States.

This is a question that cannot be ignored at the end of a study of Buddhism addressed to Christians and Jews. It would also be unwise to leave such a question unexplored in view of the fact that both Christianity and Judaism at this moment are passing through a stage of uncertainty as to the relevance of their own missionary role. There are many Christians and Jews today who are asking whether missionary work, in the sense of making converts, serves a meaningful purpose in contemporary society.

Strange as it may sound, the study of Buddhism, far from undermining the Christian and Jewish missionary position, could rather enhance it by bringing Christians and Jews to a new realization of the contemporary relevance of their mission. For that, of course, they first have to understand missionary outreach in its correct sense. Missionary work could not serve any valid purpose in the modern world if taken in the misconstrued sense of converting or bringing persons from one religion to another. The purpose of missionary work is rather to bring an individual from a state of mental childishness to a state of mental adulthood. An adult is one who faces life realistically, and continually strives to achieve the ideal humanhood for which life is designed. The work of the missionary is thus the work of helping persons to be adults, technically called in Buddhism *arahats*, in Judaism *zaddikim*, and in Christianity saints.

If missionary work is seen in that perspective, its importance and its relevance to modern society become self-evident. If the goal of missionary work is personality transformation, then there has probably been no era in the history of humankind in which it was more urgently needed than today. Purely in terms of the present world population, there has never been such a great number needing education in personality uplift.

But for missionary work of that type to be effective, missionaries, be they Buddhist, Jewish, or Christian, have to be guided by a broadened vision. They dare not be insular in their approach to religious truths. They cannot claim to have a total monopoly over the truth of an individual's path to spiritual nobility. They must be

173

prepared to admit that if they have their own techniques for personality uplift, others have other, also valid, techniques.

Therefore Christians, Jews, and Buddhists need not compete with each other. They could rather collaborate. Missionary work, or the work of educating human beings to adulthood, is a task that Jews, Christians, and Buddhists can labor at hand in hand. The very extensiveness of the task in the contemporary world would justify such a collaboration.

Modern Christian missionaries should not be taken aback if, as a result of such collaboration, they would one day come across individuals who, after successfully benefiting from the techniques of both religions, would want to consider themselves Buddhist-Christians or Christian-Buddhists. Nor should Jews be surprised at finding persons who wish to be known as Jewish-Buddhists or Buddhist-Jews. It is quite possible that as forms of personality uplift the systems of the Judeo-Christian and the Buddhist traditions have elements that are complementary to each other. It could well be that contemporary human beings need both peace of mind and self-fulfillment achieved through an active commitment to societal development, both a sense of self-dependence and a sense of relationship, both a life of self-control and a correctly oriented emotional life.

The likelihood that individuals will profit from both systems is thus not inconsiderable. If such a development takes place, neither the Buddhist, nor the Jew, nor the Christian has a right to object to it, for Gautama is not the exclusive monopoly of Buddhists, nor are the prophets and Rabbis of Jews, nor Yeshua of Christians.

Such an eventuality will not disturb a Christian or a Jew who understands religion and its function in the way that Yeshua and the Rabbis understood it. For Yeshua and the Rabbis, religion was not an end in itself. This is a point that is often overlooked, but which a modern Christian and a modern Jew will do well to remember.

174

Men and women and their growth to full humanhood were more important to the Rabbis and to Yeshua than was the religious system or the institution. That is why they opposed the attitude of those who tried to enslave others by religion. That is what they boldly insinuated when they declared: "The Sabbath is for human beings and not human beings for the Sabbath" (Mark 2:27). "The Sabbath is committed to you; you are not committed to the Sabbath" (*Mekilta*, 31.13, 14 [Smith, 1381). The Sabbath or the weekly observance of the holy day was in the popular Jewish mind the most binding practice of Judaism. It was symbolic of the entire Jewish legal system. It represented what many Jews understood by religion. So, by those statements, Yeshua and the Rabbis implied that religion should serve humanity, not enslave it. Human beings, not religion, was what was important to the Rabbis and Yeshua.

Gautama expressed the same idea when he compared religion to a raft that carries a person from one shore to another (MN, Sutta 22). Once the shore is reached, he said, travelers should not carry the raft on their head!

Thus, for Gautama, Yeshua, and the Rabbis what mattered most was the mission of religion, not religion as such. If that was the view of the founders of these religions, would it be right for their followers to accept a different view? And finally, if there is an affinity among these religions with regard to their mission, would it not be more in keeping with the desires of the founders that their adherents collaborate in the execution of this vital mission?

Works Cited

Billerbeck, Paul, *Kommentar zum Neuen Testament aus Talmud und Midrasch*, Munich, 1922.

Buddhadasa Thera, *Buddha Dhamma for Students*, Bangkok, Sublime Life Mission, 1966.

____. *Christianity and Buddhism* (Sinclair Thomson Memorial Lecture, 5th series), Bangkok, Sublime Life Mission, 1967.

____. *Two Kinds of Language: Dhammic Language, Language of the One who Knows, Human Language, Language of the One who Knows Not*, Bangkok, Sublime Life Mission, 1974.

Bury, J. B., *History of the Papacy in the 19th Century*, New York, Schocken, 1964.

Cobb, John, Jr., *To Pray or Not to Pray*, Nashville, The Upper Room, 1974.

Fazdar, Jamshed K., *The God of Buddha*, New York, Asia Publ. House, 1973.

Fisher, Eugene, *Faith without Prejudice*, New York, Paulist, 1977.

Flannery, Austin, ed., *Vatican Council II*, Collegeville, Minn., Liturgical Press, 1975.

Ling, Trevor, *The Buddha*, Harmondsworth , Middlesex, Pelican, 1976.

Peale, Norman Vincent, *The Power of Positive Thinking*, Englewood Cliffs, N.J., Prentice Hall, 1956.

Piyadassi Thera, *Buddha's Ancient Path*, London, Rider, 1964.

Powell, John, *A Reason to Live, A Reason to Die*, Niles, Ill., Argus Communications, 1972.

Punnaji Thera, M., *Beyond the Horizon of Time*, Colombo, Sri Lanka, Public Trustee Dept.

Radhakrishnan, Sarvepalli, *The Principal Upanishads*, New York, Harper and Row, 1953.

Schmidt, Karl Ludwig, "Basileia," in Gerhard Kittel, *Theological Dictionary of the New Testament*, Grand Rapids, Eerdmans, 1964.

Silva, Lynn de, *The Problem of the Self in Buddhism and Christianity*, Colombo, Sri Lanka, Ecumenical Institute, 1975.

Smith, Morton, *Tannaitic Parallels in the Gospels*, Philadelphia, Society of Biblical Literature, 1951.

Sumangala Thera, Kannimahara, "The Tradition Needs Review: An Examination of Possibilities of Refining Theravada Interpretation," in John Ross Carter, ed., *Religiousness in Sri Lanka*, Colombo, Marga Institute, 1978.

Tillich, Paul, "The Religious Symbol," *Journal of Liberal Religion*, 2 (1940).

Whitehead, Alfred North, *Religion in the Making*, New York, New American Library, 1974.

Footnotes

[1] I did this to some degree in a paper prepared for an international ecumenical symposium held in Tübingen, W. Germany, May 23-26, 1983, on the theme "Ein neues Paradigma von Theologie?"

[3] For an analysis of such investigations, see Lynn de Silva, *Re-Incarnation in Buddhist and Christian Thought*, Colombo, Sri Lanka, Ecumenical Institute, 1978.

[4] The Theravada thesis is found in the well-known Buddhist classic "Milindapanha" (see *Milinda's Questions*, 2 vols., translated by I. B. Horner, *Sacred Books of the Buddhists*, vols. 22-23, 1963). The book contains a dialogue, traceable to the days of Greek domination in India, conducted by a Buddhist monk named Nagasena, and a Greek monarch named Milinda (or Menander). This book can be said to represent an attempt to adapt the Buddhist doctrine to the thought patterns of Greek philosophy. From the point of view of the art of debate, this is a very pleasant book to read. But its no-soul doctrine does not represent the no-self doctrine of Gautama given in the "no-self" sermon. Any reader of the two texts will realize that there is a difference between Gautama's approach to the "no-self" and Nagasena's approach to the "no-soul," even though their lines of argumentation, when taken superficially, have some resemblance. Nagasena's main thought is that, apart from the Five Aggregates, there is nothing in an individual that could be called a soul. To prove his point, he uses the symbol of a chariot. When the different parts of a chariot, such as the wheels, the frame, and the yoke, are dismantled,

nothing else remains. There is no "soul" of the chariot. The five aggregates constitute the human being in the same way. There is nothing apart from the five aggregates that can be called a soul. Gautama's message is very different. His purpose in referring to the aggregates is not to show that apart from them there is nothing called a soul. He only asks his listeners not to identify any single aggregate with the "self." In fact, he is saying that the true Self (not the same thing as soul) is to be found apart from the aggregates.

⁵ The Theravada scriptures even give the impression that Buddhism is a form of monasticism meant exclusively for males. The story of the institution of the order for nuns given in the Theravada tradition tries to impress on the reader the idea that, though the order was founded by Gautama, it was done unwittingly by him and purely under pressure by Rev. Ananda, a close associate of his. See VP/CV, 254f., chap. 10, 1:1-6.

⁶Among the most important are the Sigalovada Sutta (instructions to the young Sigala), Parabhava Sutta (instructions on depravities), and Mangala Sutta (instructions on propitious signs).

⁷For a more detailed study of this sermon, see Soma Thera, *Removal of Distracting Thoughts*, Kandy, Buddhist Publication Society, Wheel Series 21, 1961.

⁸*Appamada—literally*, "nonnegligence"—is often used by Gautama in the same sense as *sati* (attentiveness).

⁹*Talmud Shabbath*, 153a; *The Babylonian Talmud*, London, Soncino Press, 1938, Shabbath, II, 781.

¹⁰The teachings of the Pharisees and Yeshua were very similar (see Leonard Swidler, "The Pharisees in Recent Catholic Writing," *Horizons*, Pall, 1983, 267-87). The Pharisee in this parable represents a distortion of the Pharisaic teachings. That distorted image tells us more about the anger of Matthew writing in 85 A.D. than of Yeshua in 30 A.D.

¹¹Jews and Christians are generally surprised to be told that God is referred to in feminine imagery in the Bible. For a collection and exegesis of such passages, see Leonard Swidler, *Biblical Affirmations of Women*, Philadelphia, Westminster, 1979.

[12]The name of the rich man is not mentioned in the Gospel, but the Latin adjective *dives*, "rich," came to be taken for his name, and he became "Dives."